THE BIG
BOOK OF MOD PODGE®

LARK

New York

An Imprint of Sterling Publishing
1166 Avenue of the Americas
New York, NY 10036

Photography by Steve Carrell
Illustrations by Orrin Lundgren

ISBN 978-1-4547-0869-8

Distributed in Canada by Sterling Publishing
c/o Canadian Manda Group, 664 Annette Street
Toronto, Ontario, Canada M6S2C8
Distributed in the United Kingdom by GMC Distribution Services
Castle Place, 166 High Street, Lewes, East Sussex, England BN7 1XU
Distributed in Australia by Capricorn Link (Australia) Pty. Ltd.
P.O. Box 704, Windsor, NSW 2756, Australia

For information about custom editions, special sales, and premium and corporate purchases, please contact Sterling Special Sales at 800-805-5489 or specialsales@sterlingpublishing.com.

Every effort has been made to ensure that all the information in this book is accurate. However, due to differing conditions, tools, and individual skills, the publisher cannot be responsible for any injuries, losses, and other damages that may result from the use of the information in this book.

Manufactured in China

1 2 3 4 5 6 7 8 9 0

larkcrafts.com

THE BIG BOOK OF MOD PODGE®

DECOUPAGE MADE EASY

New York

PROJECTS

IT'S ART! MOD PODGE MIXED MEDIA

FURNITURE FACELIFTS

RETRO REVIVAL

HANDMADE CREATIONS FOR HOLIDAYS AND CELEBRATIONS

Welcome to the wonderful world of Mod Podge!

If you are already an artist or crafter, you understand the joy and satisfaction that comes from creating with your hands. Decoupage—the art of decorating an object with paper or other materials, then applying a protective finish— offers a crafter endless ways of expressing creativity and personal style.

Are you passionate about fun and funky wearable art? Looking for easy kids' craft ideas? Want to update a bare wall or give new life to an old chest of drawers? Need a creative gift idea for the holidays? Mod Podge is the answer! The magic of Mod Podge is that it works beautifully across a wide range of crafting surfaces and across many crafting styles. This decoupage medium is the go-to product for crafters everywhere.

The Big Book of Mod Podge is your resource book for all things decoupage. Whether you're picking up a bottle of Mod Podge for the first time or you're a longtime fan, this all-inclusive book shows you just how simple and satisfying it is to create everything from fabulous fashions and stunning wall art to furniture and functional home accessories.

This easy-to-use book contains everything you need to know about Mod Podge, providing you with the resources and inspiration to get started. You'll learn about the uses of each Mod Podge formula, the tools you'll need for success, project surface preparation, and materials that can be decoupaged.

An extensive how-to techniques section covers the basics of working with Mod Podge, as well as advanced methods such as photo transfer, textured effects, and reverse decoupage.

You will be inspired by the project ideas in *The Big Book of Mod Podge*. Included are detailed instructions for 90-plus projects, which use various surfaces, materials, and design styles. Classic and vintage looks, modern ideas for home decor and fashion, upcycled furniture, and repurposed "found" surfaces are just a few of the new, inspirational ideas you'll find to help jump-start your creativity.

Some of the industry's most talented and well-known designers have contributed their ideas to this book. The unique styles of the artists— which range from traditional techniques to modern applications and beyond—highlight the amazing versatility of Mod Podge. The designs featured here use countless project surfaces and decoupage materials—paper, fabric, canvas, wood, glass, metal, and more.

Jump in and experience the wonderful world of Mod Podge crafting! Let this book be your guide to exploring the many opportunities for expressing your creativity.

STORY OF MOD PODGE

Jan Wetstone, Inventor

Mod Podge was created in 1967 by an Atlanta, Georgia, resident, Jan Wetstone. Jan, an antique and interior design shop owner, kept up with the trends. Decoupage was all the rage, yet it was an extremely time-consuming art form, as it was a tedious task to brush on multiple layers of varnish, allowing drying time and sanding between each coat. In an effort to create a less time-consuming way to decoupage, Jan began experimenting in her garage, creating her now-famous formula. As she worked to formulate a new decoupage medium, Jan tested it on a variety of surfaces. Her most famous decoupaged surface was a Volkswagen Beetle car, which she decoupaged with bedsheets. Mod Podge was born! The name Mod Podge is short for "modern decoupage."

Jan immediately began creating Mod Podge–coated prints for her shop, and they were very well received. Before long, her customers demanded that she share her decoupage secret. Well, the rest is history! Jan created Mod Podge kits, which she sold in her shop that quickly became a huge success, so successful that a major Atlanta-based department store purchased exclusive rights to her kits.

In 1979, Mod Podge found a new home with PLAID Enterprises. Since those early days of Mod Podge, several new and different formulas have been created and added to the original Matte and Gloss formulas. Additional Mod Podge family members are Satin, Fabric, Outdoor, Hard Coat, Paper, Brushstroke, Sparkle, and Antique Matte. Newer Mod Podge varieties include Mod Podge Furniture (in three different finishes), Dishwasher-Safe, Wash Out for Kids, Extreme Glitter, Ultra Matte Chalk, Clear Chalkboard Topcoat, Pearl, and Glow-in-the-Dark.

Since its invention, Mod Podge has been enjoyed by millions of crafters and do-it-yourself enthusiasts around the world. Sadly, Jan Wetstone passed peacefully in February 2013. She was loved by many and will always be acknowledged as the inventor of Mod Podge.

Through the Years

Mod Podge Today

Mod Podge today is on a fast track with a fast-growing fan base. Crafters and DIY enthusiasts of all ages love working with Mod Podge. There are inspirational photos and projects posted online every day on many blogs, websites, and social media sites such as Pinterest, showing work created by crafters who want to share their enthusiasm for the product.

As a product, Mod Podge even has its own dedicated blog, *Mod Podge Rocks!* (modpodgerocks.com), created by Amy Anderson. Every day Amy provides decoupage inspiration to "rock your world." *Mod Podge Rocks!* is jam-packed with all sorts of creative content, phenomenal projects, helpful tips, and tidbits for crafters of every level, from the novice to the experienced crafter. It was voted one of the top 50 craft blogs by Babble in 2011 and 2012, and it won the Bloggies 2014 award for the BestArt, Craft or Design Weblog. With over a million followers, *Mod Podge Rocks!* and Amy help to spread decoupage enthusiasm.

Amy is also the author of the first Mod Podge book, *Mod Podge Rocks! Decoupage Your World*, and is a contributor to this book.

FORMULA OVERVIEW

What Is Mod Podge?

Mod Podge is truly an amazing product. It has been around in the craft industry for over 45 years. It is an all-in-one glue, sealer, and finish commonly used as a decoupage medium, well loved by the novice as well as the professional crafter/artist. At its inception in the 1960s, Mod Podge was available in two original formulas, which offered crafters the choice of Mod Podge Matte or Mod Podge Gloss finishes. Since then, Mod Podge has been developed into a variety of formulas, each offering its own special finish.

Mod Podge is a brushable white medium that works beautifully when adhering paper and fabric to almost any surface. It also works as a sealer and finish. As it is brushed over a project surface, it appears milky white, yet it dries quickly to a clear, durable finish that seals and protects. Mod Podge is both versatile and dependable.

Why Different Formulas?

Over the years, Mod Podge has been developed into a variety of formulas, offering crafters and artists alike a wide variety of finishes. To this day, the most popular finishes are Mod Podge Matte and Mod Podge Gloss. However, Mod Podge has also been formulated into Mod Podge Satin, Hard Coat, Fabric, Outdoor, Paper, Sparkle, Extreme Glitter, Antique Matte, Wash Out for Kids, Super Gloss, Furniture, Dishwasher-Safe, Glow-in-the-Dark, Ultra Matte Chalk, Clear Chalkboard Topcoat, and Pearl.

Although some Mod Podge formulas were developed to work specifically on different types of surfaces or with different materials, each formula of Mod Podge also provides a different finish or look to your project. Let's explore the world of Mod Podge formulas and finishes.

CLASSIC MOD PODGE MATTE AND MOD PODGE GLOSS

The classic Mod Podge Matte and Mod Podge Gloss are your basic go-to finishes. These formulas have been around the longest. As each name implies, the Matte formula (with the yellow label) will provide your project with a nonshiny finish, and the Gloss formula (with the orange label) will offer a shiny finish to your project when dry.

Result: Each original formula is a classic, loved by all, and can be used on most surfaces with most materials. Both Mod Podge Matte and Gloss formulas are available in a variety of sizes from 2 ounces (59 mL) to a gallon (3.79 L), making them easy to use on craft projects of all sizes!

MOD PODGE SATIN

The Mod Podge Satin formula was the first to be developed after the creation of Mod Podge Matte and Mod Podge Gloss. It lies somewhere in the middle between the original finishes in sheen, providing your craft project with a smooth, soft-to-the-touch satiny finish.

Result: Mod Podge Satin is the perfect formula to use on most home decor projects when you want a subtle sheen.

MOD PODGE ULTRA-MATTE CHALK

The Mod Podge Ultra-Matte Chalk formula was developed to meet current home decor trends as it dries to an ultra-matte finish similar to chalk paint finishes. It brushes on smoothly on application without visible brushstrokes on your crafting surface.

Result: When combined with Mod Podge Matte and Mod Podge Gloss, Mod Podge Ultra-Matte Chalk allows the crafter to create a project that features contrasting finishes.

MOD PODGE CLEAR CHALKBOARD TOPCOAT

Turn any crafted surface such as paint or paper into a chalkboard surface with Mod Podge Clear Chalkboard Topcoat.

Result: After decoupaging a surface smoothly with scrapbook paper, apply Mod Podge Clear Chalkboard Topcoat. The crafted project then becomes a chalkboard surface!

MOD PODGE PEARL

The Mod Podge Pearl formula was created to give any decoupage project a touch of pearl finish. Like most Mod Podge formulas, it works as a glue, sealer, and finish all in one!

Result: Immediately after Mod Podge Pearl is applied to a project surface, a touch of pearl can be seen. Additional applications will increase the pearlescence of your project.

MOD PODGE HARD COAT

The Mod Podge Hard Coat formula was developed to provide your projects with an extra durable, protective finish, making it the perfect formula for frequently used and functional pieces, such as bookshelves and furniture.

Result: Mod Podge Hard Coat will enhance the durability of your home decor projects. When creating a home decor project, you apply not only your time but your effort too. Using Mod Podge Hard Coat will enhance your project's durability, providing you with confidence in its sustainability.

MOD PODGE FABRIC

This member of the Mod Podge family was developed to be the best fabric-to-fabric decoupage medium. It can also be used when applying fabric to hard surfaces such as metal filing cabinets or wood furniture. Mod Podge Fabric is also perfect when working with cut fabric shapes. Simply apply Mod Podge Fabric to the fabric, allow it to dry, and then cut out the fabric shapes, which will have no frayed edges, as they are now sealed. When cured, Mod Podge Fabric projects are permanent and can be hand washed when needed.

Result: Mod Podge Fabric is the best to use when decoupaging fabric-to-fabric, fabric to other surfaces, and when working with cut fabric shapes. It will adhere the fabric to a surface, seal it, and provide a finish without frayed fabric edges.

MOD PODGE OUTDOOR

Mod Podge Outdoor is perfect for all outdoor projects. It will seal a variety of surfaces—wood, tin, terra-cotta, slate, and more. It also works well on materials such as paper, fabric, and paint, providing a protective finish from rain and shine.

Result: Use Mod Podge Outdoor when creating projects that will "live" outdoors, such as birdhouses, terra-cotta flower-pots, house number plaques, and garden furniture. Mod Podge Outdoor will protect your projects for their outdoor living.

MOD PODGE PAPER

Mod Podge Paper is the perfect formula for creating a paper-to-paper project. Mod Podge Paper has been formulated to be acid-free and provides archival qualities for your paper and scrapbook-type projects, as it is nonyellowing and will help extend the life of your project. Mod Podge Paper is available in two finishes—Matte and Gloss—and dries to a smooth finish.

Result: Mod Podge Paper is the perfect formula for that discerning crafter or artist who wants to achieve archival quality. It is the best formula for creating cards, scrapbooks, mixed media, and altered art.

MOD PODGE SPARKLE

When you want to add extra glimmer to your project, Mod Podge Sparkle is the formula for you, as it contains two different sizes of holographic glitter mixed right in. Whether you brush on one light application or add a few more, Mod Podge Sparkle will add glitter sparkle effects to your project. The more applications, the more sparkle you achieve.

Result: Mod Podge Sparkle dries to a shiny, sparkly finish, which is perfect for holiday crafts, jewelry and fashion accessories, and just about any surface that needs a little extra sparkle and bling.

MOD PODGE EXTREME GLITTER

Mod Podge Extreme Glitter is made with three different holographic glitters and dries with a gloss finish. You will love using this Mod Podge formula when your project needs lots of sparkle.

Result: Mod Podge Extreme Glitter is perfect when you want to add a lot of glamour and glitz to items such as fashion, jewelry, and holiday projects.

MOD PODGE ANTIQUE MATTE

Looking for a glue and finish that will provide an antiqued look to your project? Well, this Mod Podge formula does the trick. Mod Podge Antique Matte will provide a vintage feel to your projects, creating a slightly aged look.

Result: This formula has a built-in yellow tint that is subtle. Use Mod Podge Antique Matte when you desire a warm antique or vintage effect.

MOD PODGE WASH OUT FOR KIDS

What Mom doesn't wish to have a barrel of this product around? This formula is awesome when crafting with little ones. As you may already know, other formulas of Mod Podge do not wash out of clothing. Moms and teachers alike love the Wash Out for Kids formula, since it will wash out of clothes in the washing machine with no presoaking required. So gather your little ones and begin decoupaging!

Result: This formula was created with crafty kids in mind. Mod Podge Wash Out for Kids is perfect, as it washes out of clothing and off furniture with a simple soap-and-water cleanup.

MOD PODGE SUPER GLOSS

Unlike other Mod Podge formulas, Mod Podge Super Gloss is a finish and sealer and not a glue. Used as a final topcoat, it provides an extra-thick, glass-like finish. Mod Podge Super Gloss brushes onto your project surface smoothly and dries to an ultra-clear finish without visible brushstroke marks.

Result: Mod Podge Super Gloss is a finish and sealer and provides an extra-thick, glass-like finish in one coat—without visible brush strokes. It dries ultra-clear and gives an ultra-dramatic effect.

MOD PODGE FURNITURE

Repurposing is a hot trend! Resurrect used furniture and thrift store furniture finds with easy-to-create decoupage designs using Mod Podge Furniture. This formula provides an extra-durable finish and is perfect for all furniture, such as bookshelves, tables, chairs, and kitchen accessories. Mod Podge Furniture is available in three finishes to satisfy all crafters: Matte, Satin, and Gloss.

Result: Mod Podge Furniture was created with the DIYer in mind. It's available in larger sizes, which makes it perfect for all home decor projects.

MOD PODGE DISHWASHER-SAFE

Have you ever wished you could create a decoupage project and be able to wash it in the dishwasher? Well, now you can. Use Mod Podge Dishwasher-Safe on washable surfaces such as glass, ceramics, and metal. When cured, your projects can be washed on the top shelf of the dishwasher.

Result: Mod Podge Dishwasher-Safe is perfect for indoor and outdoor use, as it dries to a very hard finish. It can be used on all washable surfaces, and the best part is that it is top-shelf dishwasher safe once cured.

MOD PODGE GLOW-IN-THE-DARK

Want to add a little extra glow to your project? Now you can! The more coats of Mod Podge Glow-in-the-Dark you add and the longer you charge the finish by placing it in direct sunlight or lighting, the longer your project will glow.

Result: Mod Podge Glow-in-the-Dark is a glue, sealer, and finish that glows and is perfect for Halloween projects. Once it has been decoupaged and cured, set your project in direct sunlight or lighting to charge the glow.

MOD PODGE DIMENSIONAL MAGIC

When your creative projects need just a little more pizzazz, use Mod Podge Dimensional Magic! This product is perfect to use when creating jewelry and scrapbooking projects with embedded charms or small trinkets. Dimensional Magic adds dramatic definition and is perfect for creating a mosaic effect. The original formula is Clear, but you will also enjoy using Sepia to create an antique or vintage look, or Glitter Gold to create glittery effects.

Result: Dimensional Magic is easy to use when applied directly from its writer-tip bottle. It adds a dimensional epoxy-like accent to your craft surface. It is milky in color when wet, yet it dries clear. Dimensional Magic is a finish topcoat only.

MOD PODGE SHEER COLORS

Want to add a tint of color to your project? Mod Podge Sheer Colors will do just that. Available in eight colors, this formula gives a transparent hue to glass and other craft surfaces. It can be applied by brush or swirled on in a container, perfect for that bright transparent color accent.

Result: After application and while wet, Mod Podge Sheer Colors are solid and milky in color—but wait. As they dry, a beautiful sheer, transparent, vivid color appears. This formula is perfect on glass, but also works beautifully as a stain for raw wood, metal and other surfaces.

MOD PODGE PHOTO TRANSFER MEDIUM

Mod Podge Photo Transfer Medium is a fabulous product that allows you to transfer your favorite image—whether it is a photograph, logo, or text—to most crafting surfaces, such as wood, fabric, canvas, terra-cotta, and metal, using either a black-and-white or color photocopy of the image.

Result: Simply apply Mod Podge Photo Transfer Medium uniformly on the face of a photocopied image, flip the image, and apply it to your crafting surface. Press it in place and allow 24 hours for it to dry. Rub over the white paper backing with a moistened sponge to remove backing. Voilà! Your image has been transferred.

MOD PODGE STIFFY

Mod Podge Stiffy is the original fabric stiffener. It allows you to stiffen fabric, ribbons, lace, needlework, and doilies for all your crafting needs. It's perfect when you want to add a little dimension to your projects.

Result: Creating stiffened doily bowls, light globes, fabric-draped sculptures, and seasonal Halloween ghosts made from cheesecloth has never been easier. Immerse your fabric in Stiffy, squeeze out excess, and place fabric over mold to dry. Easy as one–two–three!

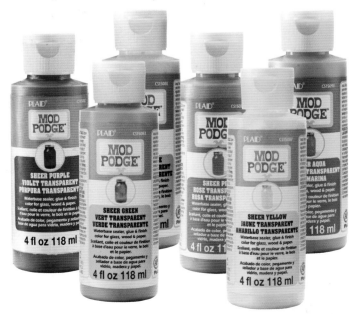

MOD PODGE WONDER GLUE

Truly a wonder glue, Mod Podge Wonder Glue works with glass, metal, ceramic, wood, and fabric. It is waterproof, paintable, and is safe for photos. Mod Podge Wonder Glue is perfect for detailed jewelry crafting or whenever you need an industrial-strength clear adhesive.

Result: Whether you need to glue together small, intricate crafted pieces or large surfaces, Mod Podge Wonder Glue is the adhesive for all your crafting needs.

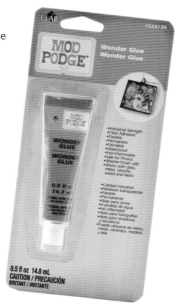

MOD PODGE MOD MOLDS AND MOD PODGE MOD MELTS

Embellishing your Mod Podge craft projects has never been easier! Do-it-yourself embellishments are fun when you use Mod Podge Mod Melts, Mod Podge Mod Melter (see page 19), and Mod Podge Mod Molds. Melting the Mod Podge Mod Melt into the durable silicone Mod Podge Mod Mold is easy. Within moments you can pop out your embellishment, which can be decorated with a wide variety of crafting supplies such as paint, stain, Mod Podge Sheer Colors, alcohol inks, and even nail polish. Craft personalities Cathie Filian and Steve Piacenza are the creators of the Mod Podge Mod Melter, Mod Podge Mod Melts, and Mod Podge Mod Molds. Read their bios on page 235.

Result: Do-it-yourself embellishments have never been easier and more fun than now. With a wide variety of colored Mod Podge Mod Melts and silicone Mod Mold designs, the crafting options are limitless.

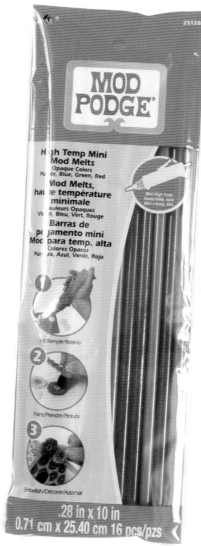

MOD PODGE COLLAGE CLAY

Get the decoden look with Mod Podge Collage Clay. Mod Podge Collage Clay, a lightweight whipped clay, packaged in a piping bag along with a variety of decorating tips, is easy to use to decorate a wide variety of crafting surfaces. Its consistency when wet is soft enough to embed decorated Mod Melt embellishments and gems (among other things), yet sturdy enough to suspend them in the clay. You will notice that the clay will begin to harden on top after several minutes; however, allow 48 hours for your project to completely dry.

Result: Mod Podge Collage Clay is fun for all ages. Squeeze to apply the clay onto your crafting surface, then embed decorated Mod Podge Mod Melt embellishments; add Mod Podge Collage Drizzle Paint and Mod Podge Podgeable Glitter and you have created a dimensional collaged masterpiece. Decorate your cell phone case, a photo frame, or a box lid—the sky's the limit.

MOD PODGE COLLAGE DRIZZLE PAINT

Top off your Mod Podge Collage Clay projects with a drizzle of paint, creating that extra drama and trim for your collaged project. Mod Podge Collage Drizzle Paint is available in four colors, which will coordinate with all your embellished designs.

Result: Whether you are creating a dimensional collaged frame, a cell phone case, jewelry, or a decorative home accent, Mod Podge Collage Drizzle Paint will add that perfect extra touch of dripped icing to your project.

MOD PODGE PODGEABLE GLITTERS

Adding that extra sparkle and glitter to a craft project has never been easier. When using Mod Podge Podgeable Glitters, you can direct the nozzle tip exactly where you want the extra sparkle. By lightly squeezing the tube, you can apply the exact amount desired.

Result: Grab your Mod Podge Podgeable Glitters when you want just the right amount of glitter in a specific spot. Just lightly squeeze the glitter tube and direct the nozzle tip.

MOD PODGE ROCKS! PEEL & STICK STENCILS

Creating a glittered accent for your Mod Podge projects is so much fun when you use Mod Podge Rocks! Peel & Stick Stencils and Mod Podge Podgeable Glitters.

Result: Easy to use, washable, and reusable, Mod Podge Rocks! Peel & Stick Stencils allow you to add a special touch of a patterned glitter accent to your Mod Podge projects. Simply put the stencil in place (it will cling to project surface), and apply Mod Podge through the stencil, using the Mod Podge Spouncer. While the Mod Podge is still wet, lift stencil and sprinkle glitter. Allow to dry and brush away excess glitter.

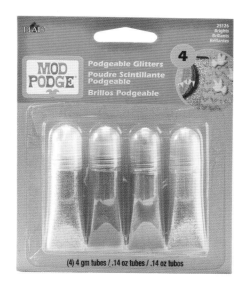

TOOLS FOR SUCCESS

Before you start crafting, you'll need to collect some supplies. We'll show you all the basic supplies you'll need—the Mod Podge Basic Tool Kit—as well as other helpful, supplementary craft tools you can add to your craft collection.

Supplementary Craft Tools

These are tools that can be very helpful when crafting, but are not requirements to complete the projects in this book. Many of these tools will add ease to your crafting experience, so here is a full list. You can add them to your tool collection as your budget permits.

- **Self-Sealing Mat.** Self-sealing or self-healing mats are usually created from a thick, durable, polyethylene plastic. They are available in a variety of sizes from a variety of manufacturers and are useful tools to have on hand. They work best as a cutting surface and are suitable for rotary cutters, utility knives, and craft knives. You will notice too that your knife blades usually last longer when you use a self-healing mat than when you cut on other surfaces.

- **Mod Podge Silicone Craft Mat.** A Mod Podge Silicone Craft Mat creates a perfect work surface and protects your work area when you craft. Not only is it easy to use, it makes cleanup quick and easy with soap and water, because nothing sticks to the surface. It's also heat resistant up to 600 degrees Fahrenheit (315.5°C), which means you can use it as your landing pad for heated tools, such as the Mod Podge Mod Melter.

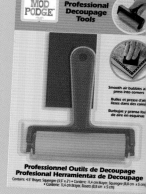

MOD PODGE BASIC TOOL KIT

- **Mod Podge.** Every project will include Mod Podge in one form or another. Specific Mod Podge formulas will be called out for each project.

- **Seven-Piece Tool Kit.** Decoupage basics in a convenient, durable, pick-me-up zippered storage pouch. Includes squeegee, 6-inch (15.2 cm) ruler, ¾-inch (19 mm) flat gold Taklon brush, 3½-inch (8.9 cm) and 6½-inch (16.5 cm) scissors, and emery board for distressing.

- **Brayer.** The Mod Podge Professional Decoupage Tool Set includes one squeegee and one brayer. A brayer is also a very useful tool to help secure decoupaged paper to the project surface and roll out excess Mod Podge medium as well as any captured air bubbles or wrinkles. After you apply paper to your project surface, and while the Mod Podge is still wet, use a brayer, beginning in the center of the paper, to apply pressure, rolling the brayer toward the paper's edges. Be sure to wipe away any excess decoupage medium that is pushed and squeezed out at the edges.

- **Squeegee.** A squeegee is helpful in securing paper to your project surface when it is too small for a brayer. The Mod Podge squeegee is useful because the edges are beveled. It's also very flexible, which enables you to apply pressure and glide across your project surface. You can access tight corners with the square edges of the squeegee.

- **Disposable Palette.** Use a disposable palette such as a foam plate when applying Mod Podge. Not only are the plates a nice work tool, they are especially perfect when cleaning up, as they can be tossed away and you can begin with a new, clean plate next time.

- **Mod Podge Spouncers.** Foam paint applicators, such as spouncers and daubers, are best used when applying paint accents over decoupaged projects by stenciling or embellishing with polka dots.

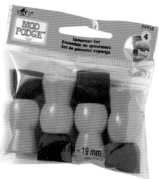

- **Paper Punches.** There are many different kinds of paper punches in the market today, offering a wide variety of designs. These are easy to use and fun when you decoupage a layered paper project.

- **Rotary Cutter.** Rotary cutters initially were created as fabric-cutting tools, but they work well for cutting large sheets of paper too. Use a rotary cutter with the help of a good ruler when long, straight cuts are desired. Keep different rotary blades for cutting fabric and paper.

- **Mod Podge Mod Melter.** The Mod Podge Mod Melter is a uniquely shaped tool that will melt the Mod Podge Mod Melts into any Mod Podge Mod Mold, creating a resin-like embellishment. The sleek design of the Mod Podge Mod Melter allows the crafter to hold the tool above the molds and fill them with ease and in their line of sight.

Helpful Hint: Use the Mod Podge Mod Melter as an all-purpose high temperature mini glue gun to make everything from molded embellishments to home decor projects, paper crafts, and more!

- **Waxed Paper.** This paper comes in handy to protect brayers, squeegee, and hands from excess Mod Podge when you press paper, fabric, and other materials in place. Position a sheet of waxed paper between your project surface and the brayer or squeegee before using these tools. This will keep excess decoupage medium from getting on the tools and will keep them clean.

- **Sandpaper.** Sandpaper comes in a variety of finishes, or grits, so we'll specify when a project requires a certain grit. It's useful for smoothing surfaces and sanding off excess paper at the edges of projects.

- **Paintbrushes.** Detail brushes are good for applying paint or finishes in small areas. Broad ones are good for applying paint or finishes in large areas. Foam brushes are also often referred to as "sponge brushes" and are awesome for decoupaging. Foam brushes can be cleaned with soap and water and reused. Soft bristle brushes are great to use when decoupaging. They offer your project a smoother finish with fewer brush-strokes or air bubbles than foam brushes do.

- **Brush Basin.** Use a water container to rinse and clean brushes between uses.

- **Paper Towels**

- **Pencil**

- **Ruler**

- **Craft Glue.** Good white craft glue is essential to have on hand when adding dimensional embellishments to your projects. There are several on the market. Experiment and find the one you like best.

- **Scissors.** It's best to keep a variety of scissors in your tool kit. Large-blade scissors are excellent to use when cutting bold, big paper designs. Small-blade scissors with sharp points are best used when cutting smaller, more detailed designs.

- **Craft Knife.** Craft knives with good sharp blades are excellent to have in your decoupage tool kit, especially when you need to cut with precision on very delicate, intricate designs. It is best to cut on a self-sealing cutting mat or a pane of glass.

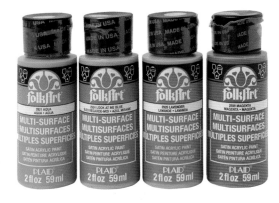

Paints

- **Acrylic Craft Paint.** Acrylic craft paints such as FolkArt Acrylic Paints, Apple Barrel Acrylic Paints, and Delta Ceramcoat Paint are all readily available in most craft stores. Acrylic craft paint is the best solution for basecoating just about any craft surface before decoupaging. These paints are created in a wide variety of colors, are inexpensive, dry quickly, and wash up with soap and water while wet.

Helpful Hint: It is best to sand your surface, then apply a basecoat, allow it to dry, re-sand, and then reapply the basecoat.

- **Spray Paint.** Spray paints are available in a wide variety of colors and finishes. Spray paint is often used on slick sealed surfaces such as metal or tinware. Always read and follow the manufacturer's instructions when spray-painting, and be sure you are working in a well-ventilated area.

- **Chalkboard Surface Paint.** Chalkboard paints are fun to use on just about any type of project, as a backdrop to your decoupaging. Read and follow the manufacturer's directions when applying chalkboard paint. However, keep in mind that when you decoupage an image onto a chalkboard surface, you should not apply Mod Podge over the entire chalkboard area, only where the images will be applied.

Helpful Hint: Be sure to condition or season the chalkboard-painted area before writing on it. To condition, rub white chalk over the entire surface, and then wipe it away. If you don't condition the chalkboard surface first, you will always see a ghost of the first written message.

Acrylic Spray Sealers

- **Mod Podge Clear Acrylic Sealers.** Acrylic spray sealers are the perfect finishes for great projects. They spray on evenly and dry quickly to provide a protective dust-resistant and fingerprint-resistant finish. Mod Podge Clear Acrylic Sealers are available in four different finishes: Matte, Gloss, Pearl, and Super Hi-Shine.

HOW TO USE MOD PODGE

If you're new to working with Mod Podge, be sure to read these instructions before beginning your project. Basic techniques will be explained, as well as how to work with a variety of surfaces and materials so you can Mod Podge seamlessly and successfully. Remember to always allow drying time between each layer of Mod Podge applied to your project. Once you've completed your project, allow for at least 24 hours of additional drying time.

Basic Decoupage Techniques

STEP ONE: PREPARING YOUR SURFACES

Different surfaces have different prep requirements, so follow the instructions here on how to prep your project surface to successfully Mod Podge.

• **Wood.** Sand wood surfaces smooth using fine-grit sandpaper. Wipe away sawdust with a moist paper towel. Apply a basecoat of paint to the surface using acrylic craft paint of choice. Allow to dry. Sand smooth once again using fine-grit sandpaper and reapply base color. Allow to dry.

• **Metal / Tin.** Wash metal and tin surfaces well with soap and water. Rinse well and dry thoroughly. Moisten a paper towel with white vinegar and wipe over cleaned metal surface to remove any remaining grease, dirt, or soap residue. Allow to dry. Basecoat paint using either brush on acrylic craft paint or spray paint. Allow to dry. Continue applying basecoat until opaque coverage is achieved. Allow to dry.

• **Glass / Sealed Ceramics.** Wash with soap and warm water. Rinse well and dry thoroughly. Moisten a paper towel with rubbing alcohol and wipe over cleaned glass or ceramic surface to remove any remaining grease, dirt, or soap residue. Allow to dry. Basecoat using FolkArt Multi-Surface paint if desired, and follow manufacturer's suggested instructions for curing the paint.

• **Terra Cotta.** Wipe clean all new terra cotta with moistened paper towel. Seal interior of pot with two or three coats of Clear Acrylic Sealer. If desired, basecoat paint exterior surface of terra-cotta pot and/or rim. Allow to dry, and reapply basecoat.

• **Papier-mâché.** Wipe clean with moist paper towel. If basecoat is desired, apply acrylic craft paint. Allow to dry. Reapply base color until desired opaqueness is reached.

• **Canvas.** Wipe primed canvas clean with a moist paper towel. If canvas is unprimed, apply a coat of gesso to prime the surface. Allow to dry, sand smooth using fine grit sandpaper and reapply a second coat of gesso.

• **Plastic.** Wash with soap and warm water; rinse well and thoroughly dry. Moisten a paper towel with rubbing alcohol and wipe over cleaned plastic surface to remove any remaining grease, dirt, or soap residue. Allow to dry.

STEP TWO: PREPARING YOUR MATERIALS

Like surfaces, different materials also require different preparation depending upon the fragility of your material and any potential for frays and ink bleeds.

Paper

• **Tissue Paper.** Working with tissue paper can sometimes be tricky, as it is very thin and fragile. It is best to cut tissue into small shapes such as squares or rectangles. You will find it easier to work with smaller sections of tissue paper, applying one at a time to the surface, slightly overlapping the shapes. You may also experience situations in which tissue paper may fold onto itself, creating creases or wrinkles. Allow the natural creases to work for you in your design.

- **Vellum Paper.** Vellum papers are very transparent and are great to use when you are working in layers. You can print images on vellum and then decoupage a transparency look onto a project. Keep in mind: vellum paper is thin and easy to wrinkle when wet, as is tissue paper.

- **Thin Scrapbook Paper.** Of somewhat higher quality than tissue paper, scrapbook paper can also be very thin and fragile. To give the paper a little more body, thereby making it easier to work with, prepare it by lightly spray-sealing both sides of the paper with Mod Podge Clear Acrylic Sealer. Allow the paper to dry thoroughly before handling.

- **Book Pages.** Depending upon the weight of the book pages, paper preparation may not be required. If your book pages are medium to heavyweight, you most likely can use the paper immediately. If the paper weight is light and very thin, you may want to seal the backside of the book page with a light coat of white spray paint. That gives the book page more stability as well as protects and seals the type so that it does not bleed through the thin paper once it has been decoupaged.

- **Magazine Pages.** Typical glossed magazine pages can be used immediately without any preparation.

- **Thick Cardstock or Scrapbook Pattern Papers.** A trick used when working with a thicker paper, especially if you are trying to cover a surface with a curve, is to moisten the paper first with water. A few helpful tips: Keep a pump bottle with water nearby to lightly spray both sides of the paper with water before coating with Mod Podge. This will give the paper a more flexible feel and will allow more "give" while working on a curve. Also keep a small container of clean water next to your work surface and dip the paper into the clean container of water, then blot on a paper towel before decoupaging. Again, the key is to prepare the paper to make it more flexible.

- **Glittered Papers.** Working with glittered papers can be fun and also a little messy. As soon as the first cut is made, it seems as though glitter gets everywhere! But that can be fun too. Use Mod Podge Sparkle when decoupaging a glittered paper, as this will not dull the glitter sparkle as the Mod Podge Matte or Mod Podge Satin might.

- **Newsprint.** Most newsprint can be used immediately without any specific preparation required. However, if your paper is very thin and/or your print is fresh ink and not yet cured, you will need to lightly spray-seal both sides of the paper to seal the newsprint ink so that it will not bleed through or blur as you work with wet decoupage medium.

Fabric

Prepare all fabrics to be decoupaged by prewashing them in mild soap and water and drying them thoroughly. Fabrics can be washed in a washing machine with commercial detergents, but fabric softeners should not be added. They can then be dried in a dryer without fabric dryer sheets. Once removed from the dryer, fabrics should be ironed to remove unwanted wrinkles, if necessary; don't use spray starch when you iron. Next, protect your work surface by using a silicone work mat or sheets of waxed paper. Lay a section of fabric over the protected work surface and begin to apply an even coat of Mod Podge Fabric using a bristle brush. You will notice that Mod Podge Fabric is full bodied and thick, so you may need to stroke and overstoke the medium to work it into and around the fabric surface. Allow the fabric to dry thoroughly to a firm and slightly shiny finish. When it is dry, you will be able to cut the fabric to the desired size needed for your project without frayed edges. This technique is also awesome when trying to cut out fabric design elements such as flowers, paisley, or children's icons to be used as the decoupaged image. Again, you will not experience any frayed edges.

Photos

First and foremost, photos to be used in a photo transfer project should be taken from your digital camera and printed, or original photographs should be photocopied. Do not use an original processed photograph. Photos can be downloaded onto your computer and manipulated using any photo processing program you have. If you are intending to use text, be sure to reverse the text so that it transfers correctly and is legible. Remember that you can size your photos to meet your specific needs during this process. Once you have completed the photo manipulation process and are ready to print your pictures, be sure to use a dry toner printer so that the ink will not smear during your crafting process. Laser printers work best, and some inkjet printers work well, however you should experiment with your printer first. If your inkjet printer smears your photograph, have it copied on a photocopy machine.

Embellishments

Embellishments to decoupage projects can encompass a wide variety of craft goods such as buttons, ribbons, lace, gems, rhinestones, small wood pieces, small found objects, buckles, jewelry, studs, and seashells. Most embellishments are added to projects in their original state; however, if you want to fashion them into another form or paint them a different color prior to attaching them to your decoupage project, feel free to do so. Be creative!

STEP THREE: PLAN YOUR DESIGN

Now that you know a little bit about all the different Mod Podge formulas and how you can use each one on different surfaces and materials, just exactly how do you plan a project from start to finish? First begin by selecting your surface, paint colors, and paper or fabric patterns and the Mod Podge formula you want to use. You might also select dimensional embellishments, if desired. Gather your Mod Podge Basic Tool Kit, materials, and any additional tools you need, and you're now ready to start crafting.

STEP FOUR: ADHERE YOUR MATERIALS

Using the Mod Podge formula you've selected for your materials, apply a coat of Mod Podge to your surface and begin adhering your materials. Since you are layering your pieces together, always start from the bottom layer and work your way up, allowing for drying time between each application of Mod Podge coating. Use the brayer and squeegee to press out any air bubbles that are trapped between your layers and to wipe away excess Mod Podge.

TIP: *When using the Mod Podge brayer and/or squeegee, you may find it helpful to lay a sheet of waxed paper between your project and the tool. This will help keep your tools clean when excess Mod Podge is squeezed out, as it will adhere to the waxed paper and not your tool! That's good to know!*

STEP FIVE: SEAL YOUR PROJECT

The last Mod Podge step is to seal your project. Using either a foam applicator or a ¾-inch (19 mm) flat brush, apply a smooth, even application of Mod Podge over the top of the entire project. Be careful not to overstroke, as this may leave brush marks. If you desire, a second coat of Mod Podge may be applied once the first coat is dried.

NOTE: *All formulas of Mod Podge are milky white when wet and will dry to a clear finish.*

STEP SIX: ADD EMBELLISHMENTS

Do you feel like adding one last layer for visual appeal? Once your project is dry, you can add dimensional pieces—for example, flowers, buttons, rhinestones—by adhering them to the top layer of your project with craft glue or a hot glue gun.

Applying Basic Decoupage Technique

To illustrate the six basic techniques above, let's create a simple decorative wall hanging. For our sample project (see photo on page 24), we've selected a design that we can cut out and combine with other papers to collage a new design.

1   Paint a basecoat around the routed edge of the plaque using FolkArt Acrylic paints. Allow the basecoat to thoroughly dry. If desired, sand any rough edges smooth using fine-grit sandpaper, and reapply a second coat of the base color. Allow to dry.

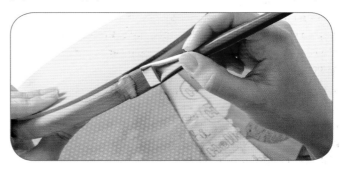

TIP: *If using a contrasting color to the paper on top, you may wish to paint just the routed edge of your crafting surface, as shown above. When painting a color matching the top paper, you may also paint just a small amount over the top of the plaque. This will color any surface edges that may show if your paper is cut too short accidentally.*

2   Cut the background paper the same oval shape as the plaque. Cut the birds, tree limb, and "Hello" bubble. This standard paper weight doesn't require additional preparation beyond cutting out the pieces to decoupage onto our wall hanging.

3   To get a visual idea of the optimum positioning of the cutout birds, tree limb, and "Hello" bubble, place the objects on the surface of the plaque. (But do not attach them!) Experiment with different arrangements. Then make a decision on what the final placement will be. Set all the cut pieces aside.

4   Using either a foam applicator or a ¾-inch (19 mm) flat brush, apply Mod Podge Matte to the wrong side of the oval paper as well as to the top of the plaque. Flip the paper over and apply it to the surface. Press in place to remove all captured air bubbles and/or wrinkles. Remove excess Mod Podge by using a Mod Podge Brayer or Mod Podge Squeegee to roll over the paper; work from the middle toward the edges. Wipe away excess Mod Podge using a dampened paper towel. Allow to dry. Continue Mod Podging the remaining paper components. Apply the tree limb and birds using the same Mod Podge techniques. Then add the "Hello" speech bubble. Allow to dry approximately 10–15 minutes before sealing the project.

5   Using either a foam applicator or a ¾-inch (19 mm) flat brush, apply Mod Podge Matte to seal your project with a final protective coat. This step will seal both the painted edge as well as the collaged papers.

6   To add a little embellishment to this project, glue dimensional silk daisies with button centers to the sealed project, as shown below. Embellishments can be glued with white craft glue, an epoxy glue, or hot glue. And there you have it, a simply beginner Mod Podge project! Wasn't that easy?

Advanced Techniques and Use of Specialty Mod Podge

PHOTO TRANSFER

Personalizing projects by transferring special photos of loved ones, favorite vacation spots, inspirational quotes, or your personal logo can change an ordinary craft project to an extraordinary project with pizzazz. There are two recommended techniques used when transferring photos: *transfer method* and *decal method*.

Transfer Method

Begin by creating a photocopy of your color or black-and-white photo. In this project, we are transferring a sweet floral heart design onto the top of a pair of girl's canvas Mary Jane shoes. (See photo on opposite page.)

TIP: *If your image contains letters or numbers, be sure to create a photocopy reversing the text. Trim excess paper from image using a pair of scissors.*

Lay a sheet of waxed paper over your work surface. Position the photocopy of the floral heart pattern right side up. Using a ¾-inch (19 mm) flat brush, apply a medium-to-thick layer of Mod Podge Photo Transfer Medium to the front of the floral heart print, making sure to cover the entire image. Clean your brush with soap and water.

Carefully lift the image with Photo Transfer Medium applied, flip the image over, and place it onto the project surface with the medium side facing down. For our project, we centered the heart design on the toe area of the shoe.

Lightly press the photo transfer image in place, beginning in the center and pressing toward the edges. The key is to make sure that the image is making contact over the entire surface without capturing air pockets or wrinkles. Allow the image to dry completely. Overnight drying is recommended.

When the image is dry, moisten the exposed paper backing with water using a small foam sponge. Allow this to set for moment and then begin lightly rubbing in a circular motion over the dampened paper. You will immediately notice the backing paper begin to roll up and peel away, exposing the floral print. Continue rubbing over the surface, removing the backing paper. Allow to dry.

Once it is dry, you may need to repeat wetting and rubbing lightly to remove excess paper if you still see some white paper fibers.

Decal Method

Photo transferring an image using the decal method is easy to do, and creating a decal is especially useful when crafting on glassware.

In this project, we are transferring a vintage styled floral bouquet to a glass apothecary jar. (See photo on page 26.)

Simply begin with a photocopy of a photograph or desired image similar to the transfer method as described above, being sure to reverse text and numbers. Trim excess paper from photocopied image.

Lay a sheet of waxed paper over your work surface. Position your photocopied image right side up on the waxed paper. Using a ¾-inch (19 mm) flat brush, apply a medium-to-thick layer of Mod Podge Photo Transfer Medium to the front of the floral bouquet photocopy, being careful to cover the entire image. Clean your brush with soap and water. Allow the image to dry completely. Overnight drying is recommended.

When the image is dry, lift it and flip it over onto a clean section of the waxed paper. Moisten the exposed paper backing with water using a small foam sponge. Allow to set a moment and then begin lightly rubbing in a circular motion over the dampened paper. You will immediately notice the backing paper begin to roll up, exposing the floral print. Continue rubbing over the surface, removing the backing paper. Allow to dry.

Once it is dry, you may need to repeat wetting and rubbing lightly to remove excess paper if you still see some paper fibers.

When satisfied that all paper fibers have been removed, you have successfully created a photo transfer decal. Carefully lift to remove the decal from the waxed paper and position where desired on your project surface. Smooth any captured air pockets or wrinkles.

DIMENSIONAL MAGIC

Adding a clear dimensional layer to projects may be just the special accent you are looking for. Mod Podge Dimensional Magic is perfect when a dimensional high-gloss epoxy-like finish is desired. Take a look at the Mod Podge frame project below. We decorated a simple square frame with painted edges, cute chevron paper, and bottle caps for dimensional embellishments. Let's see how we achieved this.

Fill / Flood an Area

Cut paper circles to fit the center bottom of the bottle caps. Apply Mod Podge to the wrong side of the paper and the bottom of the bottle cap. Apply the paper design to the bottom of the bottle cap, being careful to center it. Allow Mod Podge to dry overnight.

Once it is dry, carefully invert the Mod Podge Dimensional Magic bottle and lightly squeeze, directing the nozzle to fill the entire bottle cap. Keep bottle caps flat, and allow Dimensional Magic to thoroughly dry.

NOTE: *When wet, Dimensional Magic will be milky white and your paper image may appear hazy; however, it will dry clear and your covered image will be seen clearly again.*

Dimensional Accents

Mod Podge Dimensional Magic can be used to create dimensional accents without a frame (such as the bottle cap) as well. Simply direct the nozzle tip over the paper design such as a flower petal; it will stay where directed as long as your crafting surface is kept level while wet.

Mod Podge Super Gloss

Mod Podge Super Gloss is not to be confused with other Mod Podge formulas. It is a finish only! Apply Mod Podge Super Gloss onto your completed Mod Podged project using a ¾-inch (19 mm) flat brush. Neatly brush on a smooth coat and allow to dry. When it is dry, Mod Podge Super Gloss will provide an extra-thick glass-like finish without visible brush marks.

REVERSE DECOUPAGE

Decoupaging in reverse can be very elegant and may appear complicated; however, it is easy to accomplish one step at a time. Our project example shows a silhouette decoupaged onto the wrong side of a clear glass plate. Be sure to size the image to fit within the desired surface space. The clear glass plate is thoroughly cleaned with soap and water and then wiped down with a rubbing alcohol moistened paper towel to remove excess soap residue or any remaining impurities. Apply Mod Podge Gloss over the front of the image. Flip the image over and position where desired.

Press in place, removing air pockets or wrinkles. Allow to dry. Once dry, the backside of the glass plate can be painted a color opaquely with an acrylic paint or, in this case, with a transparent hint of color with Mod Podge Sheer Colors. Load a Mod Podge Spouncer with Mod Podge Sheer Color and begin spouncing up and down over the backside of the plate, making sure all areas are covered. Reload the spouncer when needed. Allow to dry.

If additional color is desired, a second application of Sheer Color can be applied in the same manner. Use Sheer Color projects for decorative purposes only, as they will not be dishwasher safe.

COVERING CURVED SURFACES

Mod Podging a curved surface is not as hard as you may think. Decoupaging curved surfaces is easy if you select a thinner, non-textured paper such as lightweight scrapbook papers, newspapers, gift wrap, and even tissue paper.

To make a project with a curved surface, such as a piggy bank, begin by cutting the paper into small sections.

TIP: *For tighter curves, smaller pieces work best.*

Brush a coat of Mod Podge onto both the surface as well as the wrong side of the paper.

Apply the paper to the curved object, overlapping the pieces, and allow it to dry.

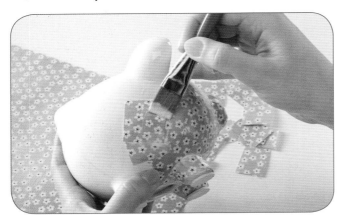

Once it is completely covered and dry, brush a coat of Mod Podge over the entire surface and embellish by adding facial features with paint, if desired.

PAINT AND STENCIL DETAILS

Decoupage can be a lot more than simply Mod Podging paper to a surface. Once a surface has been decoupaged with paper and sealed with Mod Podge, you can add to the project using stencils and paints. Take a look at the decorated cube box shown below. We added dimensional ball wood feet to the box and a dimensional wood ball knob to the lid. But notice what was done to the box sides after book pages were Mod Podged. Using a simple paper stencil taped in place, we added a painted/stenciled design. To do that, simply load the spouncer with paint, dab onto a paper towel to off-load excess paint, and begin stenciling using a dabbing up-and-down motion. Once the open area of the stencil has been painted opaquely, carefully lift the stencil to reveal the design, and repeat for each side of the box.

Beyond Decoupage

When you hear the words *Mod Podge* or *decoupage*, you often think of cut paper that is glued and sealed to a surface. But Mod Podge can be used in so many different ways to achieve different effects.

TEXTURED EFFECTS

Thin, lightweight papers such as gift wrap tissue paper is perfect for creating textured effects! Basic white tissue paper is perfect to use if you intend to paint your project when the texture decoupage technique is completed. You can also experiment by using colored tissue papers and not adding paint over the textured effects. The choice is yours. Our sample frame project here shows you how we used white tissue paper and Mod Podge to create the textured effect and then paint over it, creating a leather-like look.

To create this look, cut or tear small sections of tissue paper; crinkle the paper into a tight ball, creating deliberate wrinkles. Open the tissue paper ball without completely smoothing it out; you want some wrinkles to remain. Using a ¾-inch (19 mm) flat brush and working a small section at a time, apply a coat of Mod Podge Gloss onto your project surface. Place the wrinkled tissue paper over the wet Mod Podge and immediately brush a second coat over the wet tissue, keeping wrinkles in place. Add a second piece of wrinkled tissue next to and slightly overlapping the first. Continue until the entire project surface is covered. Allow to dry.

TIP: *Do not overwork the Mod Podge and tissue paper by overstroking. The paper is thin and will tear when wet.*

Using the same ¾-inch (19 mm) flat brush, paint textured surface desired colors. Here the red and yellow gold shades are blended, then the edges are darkened with two shades of brown. Allow to dry.

Depending on the finished sheen desired, you may brush a coat of Mod Podge Gloss over the project when the paint is dry to further seal and protect your project.

MOD PODGE SHEER COLORS

Adding a hint of color to a decoupage project is always fun. This project illustrates how Mod Podge Sheer Colors can be used to tint or add a slight hint of color to decoupaged projects. In this case, taking a simple black-and-white decoupaged print or photo and brushing Mod Podge Sheer Color over the surface brings the project to life with a light monotone color story.

Mod Podge Sheer Colors can be used to tint clear glass, ceramics, metal, wood, canvases, and many other common crafting surfaces. Mod Podge Sheer Color projects look like a color tinted milky white when wet and will dry to a vibrant hint of color that is transparent on glassware. Use Mod Podge Sheer Color projects for decorative purposes only, as they will not be dishwasher safe.

MOD PODGE COLLAGE CLAY

The art form called decoden is quickly sweeping the crafting world. Decoden is a craft whereby a whipped clay is applied to a surface and then, while it is still wet, small trinkets or embellishments are embedded into the whipped clay. The more trinkets and embellishments the better! Taking the project to the next level is easily done by drizzling paint and adding glitter, which will totally take your craft project to a decadent level!

When creating the Mod Podge Collage Clay project shown at the right, begin by basecoating the raw wood box with acrylic paint and allow it to dry.

Next, add the star decorator tip to the bag of Mod Podge Collage Clay and apply star-shaped whipped clay clusters side by side across the top of the box.

While the Mod Podge Collage Clay is still wet, Mod Podge Glitter can be added.

Still working while the Mod Podge Collage Clay is wet, you can add Mod Podge Mod Mold embellishments, as well as other trinkets or embellishments such as flat-back gems or pearls. Mod Podge Collage Drizzle Paint can be added to finish off your Mod Podge Collage Clay project. Remember to allow several days for curing, depending on how thick the clay was applied as well as how humid the climate is.

CASTING

Mod Podge and acrylic paint can be used to create a stained glass effect on glassware. This technique is called casting.

To create this effect, first pour two parts Mod Podge Gloss into a bowl. Add one part acrylic paint and begin mixing using a palette knife. Continue mixing until you no longer see swirls of color or white Mod Podge. Be careful not to "whip" air bubbles into the mixture.

Pour the mixture out of the bowl onto a Gallery Glass Leading Blank and spread in uniform thickness. (The Leading Blank is a plastic crafting surface that allows you to peel away the mixture when it is dry.) If desired, you can add texture by leaving some palette knife strokes on the surface.

TIP: *If air bubbles appear, lift the leading blank and tap the underneath side using the handle end of a paintbrush.*

Carefully replace the leading blank down on a level surface and allow to dry. Overnight drying is recommended.

Once it is thoroughly dry, cut through the dried mixture in any desired shape using a craft knife. Our sample project for this technique shows daisy petals have been cut and are being lifted from the leading blank.

TIP: *If you prefer not to cut the design freehand, prepare a pattern by drawing bold permanent ink marker lines and place the pattern underneath the Leading Blank where you can see the pattern through the cast Mod Podge mixture.*

Next, peel the cut shape from the Leading Blank and place on the glass surface where desired. Continue cutting daisy petals until a full daisy has been created. Make as many daisies as desired. This technique is intended for decorative purposes only, as it is not permanent and the glassware cannot be washed in a dishwasher; handwash only.

EXPLORING CREATIVE OPTIONS

As you begin the creative process, your inspiration will drive your Mod Podge project designs. This section offers assistance to the novice crafter and is a helpful reminder to the avid crafter, providing more reasons to create, more ways to approach a project, and a lot more inspiration.

Materials

All design materials can offer inspiration to us. Each material provides color, texture, and patterns that can drive our creativity and ignite a creative spark. The list of design materials is long. Below we list just a few.

Paper. Paper is available in many textures, weights, patterns, and colors; each delivers a different look and feel to your Mod Podge project. Paper can be sourced as manufactured paper, which offers you a trip to the paper aisle of your favorite craft store, or as recycled paper, which can provide opportunities to be "green."

Manufactured Papers. You can choose from printed scrapbook paper, paper bags, rice paper, wallpaper, tissue paper, gift wrap, and napkins, to mention just a few. The design and color choices of manufactured papers are endless.

Recycled/ Repurposed Papers. There are a multitude of "found" papers, including candy wrappers, ticket stubs, receipts, children's artwork, sewing patterns, comic books, maps, matchbooks, printed book pages, catalogs, poster art, recipes, illustrated storybooks, magazines, postage stamps, and handwritten letters. When you design with recycled papers, you are only limited by what repurposed papers you collect.

Photographs. Incorporating a photo in your Mod Podge project can offer a creative opportunity to add that personalized touch. A photo is the ideal element to use as a focal point of the project, or as part of a collage. Project designs will vary based on color, pattern, placement, and personalization. Images can be downloaded to or scanned to your computer and printed.

Embellishments. Completing a Mod Podge project with dimensional embellishments such as buttons, pins, keys, shells, board game pieces, old jewelry charms, bottle caps, sequins, rhinestones, or flat-back gems will add detail. Embellishments are perfect for the layering and texture needed for Mod Podging mixed media creations. Also try creating your own embellishments using Mod Podge Mod Melts and Mod Podge Mod Molds.

Fabrics and Trims. Using fabric as the base of your Mod Podge project, or using a trim as an embellishment, will add a sense of flair while providing color, weight, and texture. The list of fabrics and trims is endless. Try adding cotton prints, linen, lace, burlap, or canvas to your next decoupage project.

Paint. Paint is the key to most Mod Podge projects. Your addition of paint will provide not only color, but also opportunities for design pattern accents, color blocking, stenciling, and trim accents, which will enhance your Mod Podge project.

Design Techniques

Color. Color will enhance your design. The way you approach your choice of project color, and your color inspiration, can come from any of your project materials. In a sense, color can drive the reason you create a project.

Black & White. This is a totally classic look, never going out of style. Designing a project with the everlasting traditional palette of black and white or with various shades of gray in between is a perfect choice when incorporating a black-and-white photo, book pages, newsprint, or classic typography in your Mod Podge project. You can even try playing with a pop of color for an eye-catching accent to the classic black-and-white palette.

Single Color. A Mod Podge project can use only one color for a monochromatic look. However, you can also step outside of the one-color box and use a variety of shades or tints of the original color, creating a color value range, incorporating an ombré effect.

Multicolor. The use of three or more colors when designing a Mod Podge project will open up color possibilities, offering a wide range of contrast. Multicolor may be less confining than single color or black-and-white. Color inspiration will come from the materials used in a project.

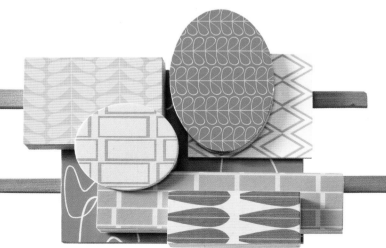

Layout Applications

These are methods or techniques that can be used to apply materials on a prepared surface, creating pattern, texture, and design in your Mod Podge project.

Single-Layer Application.
This technique is perfect for the novice as well as the avid Mod Podger who uses a single layer as a base when collaging a project. Simply cut the paper or other material in its original state, without any manipulation, to the size and shape of the project surface, and apply it directly. This project can then be embellished with painted chipboard letters, as shown here.

Cut Pieces. Pieces of paper or fabric can be cut into shapes such as strips, squares, circles, triangles, and even die-cut patterned shapes, and then assembled to create a pattern or image.

Silhouette Motifs.

Keeping things simple and designing decoupage projects with an understated elegance can be a lot of fun and so easy to do. Silhouette motifs are created opaquely in one color. Our crafted project here represents a more modern approach to the silhouette. With a decoupaged chevron-pattern paper as the background, the solid-colored cat paper silhouettes seem to pop off the crafted surface once decoupaged on top. Silhouettes can be created from any online images and, if needed, can be resized on your computer.

Torn Pieces. Tearing paper or fabric into various sizes and shapes can offer fun, decorative patterns. Tearing double-sided patterned papers will also offer edges of contrasting color and pattern. Torn-paper sections are perfect for covering three-dimensional objects that have curved surfaces.

Random Pattern. Designing with a random pattern is very free. There is no set design structure that is recognizable. This technique is perfect when Mod Podging with candy wrappers or typographic elements.

Rolled Paper. A fun technique is to create designs with rolled paper. You can use scrapbook paper, newspaper, storybook pages, maps, or even sturdy gift wrap. The fish plaque is an example of a rolled paper project. Paper was rolled around a small dowel and then Mod Podged closed. Once the Mod Podge had set, we slipped the rolled paper off the dowel rod and created several more individual rolls. Each roll was then cut to size to create our fish silhouette, and the rolls were then Mod Podged to the surface.

EXTRAORDINARY EVERYDAY CRAFTS

Here are some simple, budget-minded, beginner-friendly projects, which include easy ways to dress up everyday decor, celebrate family, and create one-of-a-kind gifts.

THE BIG

BOOK OF MOD PODGE®

VINTAGE SEWING PATTERN STORAGE BOX

DESIGNER: **Amy Anderson**

Sewing can be lots of fun, but storing your sewing projects and fabric supplies in an organized box is even better. This creative use of old sewing patterns will brighten up any sewing or craft room.

WHAT YOU'LL NEED   MOD PODGE BASIC TOOL KIT (PAGE 18); MAKE SURE YOUR CRAFT KNIFE HAS A VERY SHARP OR NEW BLADE ☐ MOD PODGE GLOSS ☐ LARGE WOOD BOX (WITH LID) ☐ TACK CLOTH (OPTIONAL) ☐ FOLKART ACRYLIC PAINT: LINEN AND BABY BLUE ☐ FOUR 2-INCH (5 CM) WOOD BALLS WITH ONE FLAT SIDE, FOR BOX FEET ☐ VINTAGE SEWING PATTERN PIECES WITH THEIR PATTERN ENVELOPES ☐ SELF-HEALING CUTTING MAT (OPTIONAL) ☐ HANDLE OF CHOICE FOR THE BOX LID ☐ MOD PODGE WONDER GLUE ☐ DRILL AND DRILL BIT TO FIT HANDLE SCREWS ☐

WHAT YOU'LL DO

1   Prepare the box by sanding, if necessary. Wipe away dust with tack cloth.

2   Paint exterior of box and lid completely, using FolkArt Acrylic Paint in Linen. Apply several coats for full coverage, allowing it to dry before applying the next coat. If desired, the interior or the box can be painted using FolkArt Acrylic Paint in Linen.

3   Paint wood balls with FolkArt Paint in Baby Blue. Apply several coats for full coverage, allowing each to dry before applying the next coat.

4   Remove tissue patterns from a pattern envelope. Trim the envelope front from the rest of the envelope with scissors. Repeat with several envelopes.

5   Mod Podge the envelope fronts onto the box lid, overlapping where desired. Do this by adding a medium layer of Mod Podge to the back of each envelope front and smoothing it onto the box lid. Repeat with remaining envelope fronts, let dry 15–20 minutes, and then add a topcoat of Mod Podge Gloss. Allow to dry.

6   Trim any excess paper that extends over the box lid by flipping the lid upside down onto a solid surface and then running a craft knife along each side.

7   Unfold the sewing pattern pieces and cut into large sections. Starting on one outer side of the box, decoupage the pattern pieces down. Do this by applying a medium layer of Mod Podge to the box surface; then smooth the pattern piece down on top. Allow to dry for 15–20 minutes.

TIP: *Smooth the tissue patterns carefully so that you don't tear your pattern pieces. It's okay if you get some wrinkles in the thin tissue; it adds to the character of the finished piece.*

8   Continue Mod Podging pattern pieces down until you have covered one entire side of the box. Allow to dry and apply a topcoat of Mod Podge. Allow to dry.

9   Trim any excess paper from the side of the box using a craft knife. Slowly run the craft knife down each edge of the box side, trimming the excess pattern pieces. Repeat this process with the other three sides of the box.

10   Apply a final layer of Mod Podge Gloss to the whole box and lid and allow to dry (A).

11   Glue the wood feet to the bottom of the box, using Mod Podge Wonder Glue.

12   Drill holes to attach the handle to the lid. Make sure to follow the instructions on the hardware packaging to attach handle.

13   Allow the box to dry for 24 hours before using.

STIFFENED DOILY BOWL

DESIGNERS: **Cathie Filian and Steve Piacenza**

Doily bowls are sweet, a little country chic, and oh so simple to make.
Fill them with wrapped candies, potpourri, or small trinkets.

WHAT YOU'LL NEED ☐ MOD PODGE STIFFY ☐ MOD PODGE SILICONE CRAFT MAT ☐ LARGE YOGURT
CONTAINER ☐ ALUMINUM FOIL ☐ SMALL MIXING BOWL ☐ LARGE COTTON DOILY ☐ MOD PODGE
MOD MELTER AND GLUE STICKS ☐ DECORATIVE ARTIFICIAL FLOWER

WHAT YOU'LL DO

1 Cover outside of the yogurt container with aluminum
foil and place container upside down on the Mod Podge
Silicone Craft Mat.

2 Pour Mod Podge Stiffy into the mixing bowl. Soak the doily in
Mod Podge Stiffy (A).

3 Remove doily from bowl and gently squeeze excess Mod
Podge Stiffy from the doily. (B).

4 Place doily over the foil-covered yogurt container, centering
wet doily so the edges are even (C).

5 Allow to dry overnight. Once dry, separate stiffened doily
bowl from yogurt container and remove any aluminum foil
that may have stuck to it.

6 Hot-glue flower embellishment to bowl using Mod Podge
Mod Melter.

Ⓐ

Ⓑ

Ⓒ

FABRIC-DECOUPAGED TERRA-COTTA FLOWERPOTS

DESIGNER: *Chris Williams*

As an avid gardener and crafter, I am always searching for fun and creative ways to highlight both skills. These fabric-decoupaged terra-cotta flowerpots are not only fabulous in the garden, but are also great for indoor storage and organization.

WHAT YOU'LL NEED   MOD PODGE BASIC TOOL KIT (PAGE 18)   ▢   MOD PODGE FABRIC   ▢   8½-INCH (21.6 CM) TERRA-COTTA FLOWERPOT   ▢   TWO 6½-INCH (16.5 CM) TERRA-COTTA FLOWERPOTS   ▢   ASSORTED SMALL-PRINT COTTON FABRICS   ▢   LARGE SHEET OF TRACING PAPER OR NEWSPAPER   ▢   BLACK MARKER WITH NARROW POINT   ▢   ASSORTED CRAFT BUTTONS   ▢   TEMPLATES: FLOWERS, LEAVES, SQUARE, CIRCLE (PAGE 229)

WHAT YOU'LL DO

1 Begin by making a paper pattern of each flowerpot. Lay a large sheet of tracing paper or newspaper down flat on the work surface. Using a pencil, trace the base and along the top rim of the flowerpot as you slowly roll it across the paper. When complete, the pattern will resemble an arch shape. Add approximately ½ inch (1.27 cm) of depth to the base curve and 2 inches (5.1 cm) depth to the top rim curve, to draw a taller flowerpot pattern. Cut out the pattern. Repeat for the second size of flowerpot.

2 Working one terra-cotta flowerpot at a time, position the paper pattern created in step 1 over one length of fabric. Cut out fabric around the paper pattern.

3 Using a ¾-inch (19 mm) flat brush, apply Mod Podge Fabric to the exterior surface of the terra-cotta flowerpot. It is easiest to work with a small section at a time. Position the fabric over the terra-cotta flowerpot, leaving some excess fabric at the bottom and top. Smooth the fabric over the Mod Podged areas, being sure to release any air pockets or fabric wrinkles. It is best to apply pressure just under the rim of the terra-cotta flowerpot to be sure the fabric is snugly pressed up against the pot. Repeat this process in sections until the entire flowerpot is covered in fabric. Once the fabric is smoothed into place without air pockets or fabric wrinkles, apply a coat of Mod Podge Fabric over the exterior.

4 Using scissors, trim the excess away at the bottom of the terra-cotta flowerpot; then set the flowerpot upright.

5 While the flowerpot is still wet, quickly make vertical cuts in the excess fabric at the top, cutting down to the rim. Apply Mod Podge Fabric just inside the flowerpot rim, then fold the excess fabric over the rim and adhere each fabric section in place; if needed, slightly overlap each fabric section.

TIP: *The cuts in the fabric will make it easier for the fabric to lie smoothly against the inside of the flowerpot.*

6 Repeat steps 2 through 5 for each flowerpot.

7 Prepare small sections of fabric to create appliqués by brushing Mod Podge Fabric directly onto the fabric. Then allow it to dry flat or over a clothesline. This fabric section will dry slightly stiff, which is a good thing, as it is always easier to cut fabric appliqués if the fabric has been Mod Podged, because it will not fray or produce any loose threads when cut into shapes.

8 With a fine-point permanent marker, trace the flower, leaf, circle, and square template patterns (page 229) onto stiff paper or cardstock, and cut out templates. On the backs of the prepared appliqué fabrics, trace around the patterns. Cut several appliqués from the prepared fabric to decoupage onto your flowerpots.

9 Brush Mod Podge Fabric on the back of each appliqué; then apply a flower, circle center, and leaves, one piece at a time, around the flowerpot bases. Apply the square shapes around the rims of the terra-cotta flowerpots.

10 When each terra-cotta flowerpot is dry, embellish with colorful craft buttons in the flower centers and around the rim, using craft glue.

NOTE: *Stacking the buttons will create additional interest.*

TIP: *For outdoor use, create flowerpots using Mod Podge Outdoor.*

GLITTERED KEYS AND KEY HOLDER

DESIGNER: **Chris Williams**

Inspire

Dream

Wish

Everyone needs a little glitter and sparkle in their lives! Why not add glitter and a few beads to your keys and keychain? I promise it will make running errands a lot more fun! As a bonus, and to assist you in keeping organized, create a key-ring holder, which can be easily mounted near a doorway.

WHAT YOU NEED   MOD PODGE BASIC TOOL KIT (PAGE 18)   ◼   MOD PODGE GLOSS   ◼   MOD PODGE DIMENSIONAL MAGIC, CLEAR   ◼   MOD PODGE PODGEABLE GLITTER, BLUE   ◼   MOD PODGE ROCKS! PEEL & STICK STENCILS, SKELETON KEY   ◼   FOLKART MULTI-SURFACE PAINTS: AQUA AND PARCHMENT   ◼ 6½ x 9½-INCH (16.5 CM x 24.1 CM) RECTANGULAR WOOD PLAQUE   ◼   3¼ x 5¼-INCH (8.3 CM x 13.3 CM) OVAL WOOD PLAQUE   ◼   ASSORTED KEYS   ◼   1½-INCH (3.8 CM) METAL JEWELRY CIRCLE BEZEL, TO HANG FROM KEY CHAIN   ◼   4 SODA BOTTLE CAPS   ◼   SCRAPBOOK PAPER, FLORAL AND POLKA DOT PATTERNS, OR YOUR CHOICE   ◼   ¾-INCH (19 MM) FLAT BRUSH,   ◼   ASSORTED BEADS AND CHARMS   ◼   3 BRASS CUP HOOKS   ◼ SILVER JUMP RINGS, EYE PINS   ◼   3 SPLIT KEY RINGS   ◼   JEWELRY TOOLS: FLAT-NOSE PLIERS, ROUND-NOSE PLIERS, SIDE-CUTTING PLIERS   ◼   MOD PODGE WONDER GLUE

WHAT YOU'LL DO

KEYS

1   Working one side of a key at a time, apply Mod Podge Gloss to the head of the key, using a ¾-inch (19 mm) flat brush (A).

2   While Mod Podge is still wet, generously sprinkle on the glitter (B). Allow to dry. Reapply both Mod Podge Gloss and glitter if necessary. Allow to dry, flip key over, and repeat for backside of key head.

NOTE: *When using Mod Podge Podgeable Glitters, remove cap, direct nozzle, point and lightly squeeze; glitter will fall where tip is directed. Unused glitter can be captured and reused.*

3   Brush a coat of Mod Podge Gloss over glittered areas to seal and protect the glitter. To add a protective gloss dimensional finish, apply Mod Podge Dimensional Magic Clear over glittered areas (C). Allow to dry; flip key and repeat on reverse side of key.

RECTANGULAR KEY HOLDER PLAQUE

1 Paint side edge of plaque with FolkArt Multi-Surface Paint in Aqua and the routed edge of plaque Parchment. Allow to dry. Sand smooth and reapply base color, if desired.

2 Measure and cut floral patterned paper to fit the top surface of the rectangular wood plaque. Apply paper to plaque using Mod Podge Gloss. Allow to dry 10 minutes and apply Mod Podge Gloss over paper to seal. Allow to dry.

3 Accent corners and edges of floral paper with FolkArt Multi-Surface Paint in Aqua to create added interest.

4 Using ¾-inch (19 mm) flat brush, apply Mod Podge Gloss over side edges of rectangular plaque. Quickly, while Mod Podge is still wet, sprinkle with glitter.

NOTE: *It may be easier to pour a small puddle of glitter onto a sheet of waxed paper and touch wet Mod Podge to the glitter rather than sprinkling glitter onto the plaque.*

OVAL PLAQUE

1 Paint side edge of oval plaque using FolkArt Multi-Surface Paint in Aqua and the routed edge and top of plaque in Parchment. Allow to dry. Sand smooth, and reapply base color, if desired.

2 Measure and cut oval from polka dot patterned paper to fit top center of plaque. Apply paper to plaque using Mod Podge Gloss. Allow to dry 10 minutes, and apply Mod Podge Gloss over paper to seal. Allow to dry.

3 Accent edges of sealed polka dot paper with FolkArt Multi-Surface Paint in Aqua to create added interest.

4 Position Mod Podge Rocks! Peel & Stick Skeleton Key Stencil in center of oval plaque. Apply Mod Podge Gloss through opening of stencil (A). While still wet, lift stencil; then sprinkle Mod Podge Podgeable Blue Glitter over wet Mod Podge (B). Allow to set, and when dry, brush away excess glitter.

5 Using ¾-inch (19 mm) flat brush, brush Mod Podge over side edges of oval plaque. Quickly, while Mod Podge is still wet, sprinkle with glitter.

NOTE: *It may be easier to pour a small puddle of glitter onto a sheet of waxed paper and touch wet Mod Podge to the glitter rather than sprinkling glitter onto the plaque.*

SODA BOTTLE CAPS AND KEY CHAIN CIRCLE BEZEL

1 Cut 1-inch (2.5 cm) circles of polka dot papers. If desired, cut a few flowers and/or leaves from floral paper and position over polka dot paper to create a collaged effect.

2 Type and print out inspirational words such as Inspire, Dream, and Wish on the computer. Make them the correct size to fit bottle caps, and cut them out.

3 Attach paper circles, floral cutouts, and words inside soda bottle caps with Mod Podge Gloss. Using FolkArt Multi-Surface Paint in Aqua, paint a light wash over printed words. Mod Podge over papers and allow to dry.

4 Fill soda bottle caps with Mod Podge Dimensional Magic Clear, and allow to dry.

5 Repeat steps 1 through 4 to create key chain circle bezel or hanging bottle cap.

CUP HOOKS

1 Using FolkArt Multi-Surface Paint in Aqua, paint brass cup hooks Aqua and allow to dry. Reapply color, if needed.

ASSEMBLY

1 Center oval plaque on top of the rectangular plaque and attach using Mod Podge Wonder Glue. Keep flat while adhesive is drying.

2 Evenly space painted cup hooks at bottom of rectangular plaque and screw into plaque.

3 Using Mod Podge Wonder Glue, attach three bottle caps with inspirational words above cup hooks.

4 Using jewelry tools, add bead charms to keys and key rings. Add jewelry circle bezel and soda bottle cap charms to key ring.

FAMILY MESSAGE BOARD AND BOTTLE CAP MAGNETS

Finding new uses for everyday items is always fun and exciting. For a very small investment, you can take an everyday metal cookie sheet and turn it into a family message board with handcrafted magnets. This project uses chalkboard paint and can be completed in an afternoon.

WHAT YOU NEED MOD PODGE BASIC TOOL KIT (PAGE 18) ☐ MOD PODGE MATTE ☐ MOD PODGE DIMENSIONAL MAGIC, CLEAR ☐ FOLKART CHALKBOARD PAINT, BLACK ☐ FOLKART MULTI-SURFACE PAINT, YELLOW OCHRE AND PUEBLO ☐ 9 x 13-INCH (22.9 x 33 CM) METAL COOKIE SHEET ☐ 3 x 2-INCH (7.6 x 5.1 CM) RECTANGULAR PAPIER-MÂCHÉ BOX ☐ FRUIT AND BUTTERFLIES SCRAPBOOK PAPER ☐ METAL SODA BOTTLE CAPS ☐ WHITE CHALK ☐ MAGNET DISCS TO FIT BACKS OF BOTTLE CAPS ☐ RUBBING ALCOHOL ☐ MOD PODGE WONDER GLUE ☐ SMALL NOTE PAPERS

WHAT YOU'LL DO

1 If using a new cookie sheet, first remove paper labels. Prepare new or used cookie sheet by washing in warm, soapy water. Rinse well and dry thoroughly. Wipe surface with a paper towel moistened with rubbing alcohol to remove any remaining grease or soap film.

2 Paint over bed of cookie sheet with FolkArt Black Chalkboard Paint. Allow to dry and reapply. Chalkboard area should be opaque, without any shiny metal showing through. A third coat may be necessary. Allow to dry; then condition painted chalkboard surface by rubbing white chalk over entire surface and wiping it off with a dampened paper towel.

3 Using FolkArt Multi-Surface Paint, paint inner sides of cookie sheet with Yellow Ochre and paint the top edge with Pueblo. Allow to dry and reapply for opaque coverage.

4 Cut desired fruit, leaves, and butterfly patterns from scrapbook paper.

TIP: *If desired, create a design that "flows" off the edge of the cookie sheet, showing only a portion of a leaf or piece of fruit. It will add more interest.*

5 Attach the paper cutouts to the chalkboard surface by applying Mod Podge Matte only to the wrong side of the paper and pressing them in place. Do not apply Mod Podge Matte on the chalkboard surface where paper will not be attached, as this will seal the chalkboard paint. Wipe away any excess Mod Podge Matte from the painted chalkboard surface while wet.

6 Measure and cut a colorful paper strip the height of the papier-mâché box, to go around it; Mod Podge the strip to the box with Mod Podge Matte. Attach a butterfly cutout to what will become the front of the box (see photo); then coat the entire box with Mod Podge Matte. Allow to dry. Set aside.

7 Using FolkArt Multi-Surface Paint, paint the inside edges of metal bottle caps with Pueblo. Allow to dry.

8 Cut 1-inch (2.5 cm) circles from colorful paper to fit inside metal bottle caps. Adhere the circles in place with Mod Podge Matte. Print family members names in a desired font from the computer or by hand, to fit inside the metal bottle caps. Cut out the names and adhere them to the bottle cap centers.

TIP: *A 1-inch (2.5 cm) circle paper punch works perfectly for cutting out circles.*

9 Once the paper circles are dry, fill the metal bottle caps with Mod Podge Dimensional Magic Clear; keep them flat and allow to dry.

10 Glue a magnet disc to the back of each metal bottle cap with Mod Podge Wonder Glue adhesive. Glue the papier-mâché box to lower edge of tray as a holder for chalk sticks. Attach a few note papers to cookie sheet with magnets and then hang it in the kitchen, using a command strip for all family members to write notes, which can be chalked on or held on with magnets.

DESK SET PHOTO CUBE

DESIGNER: ***David Cheaney***

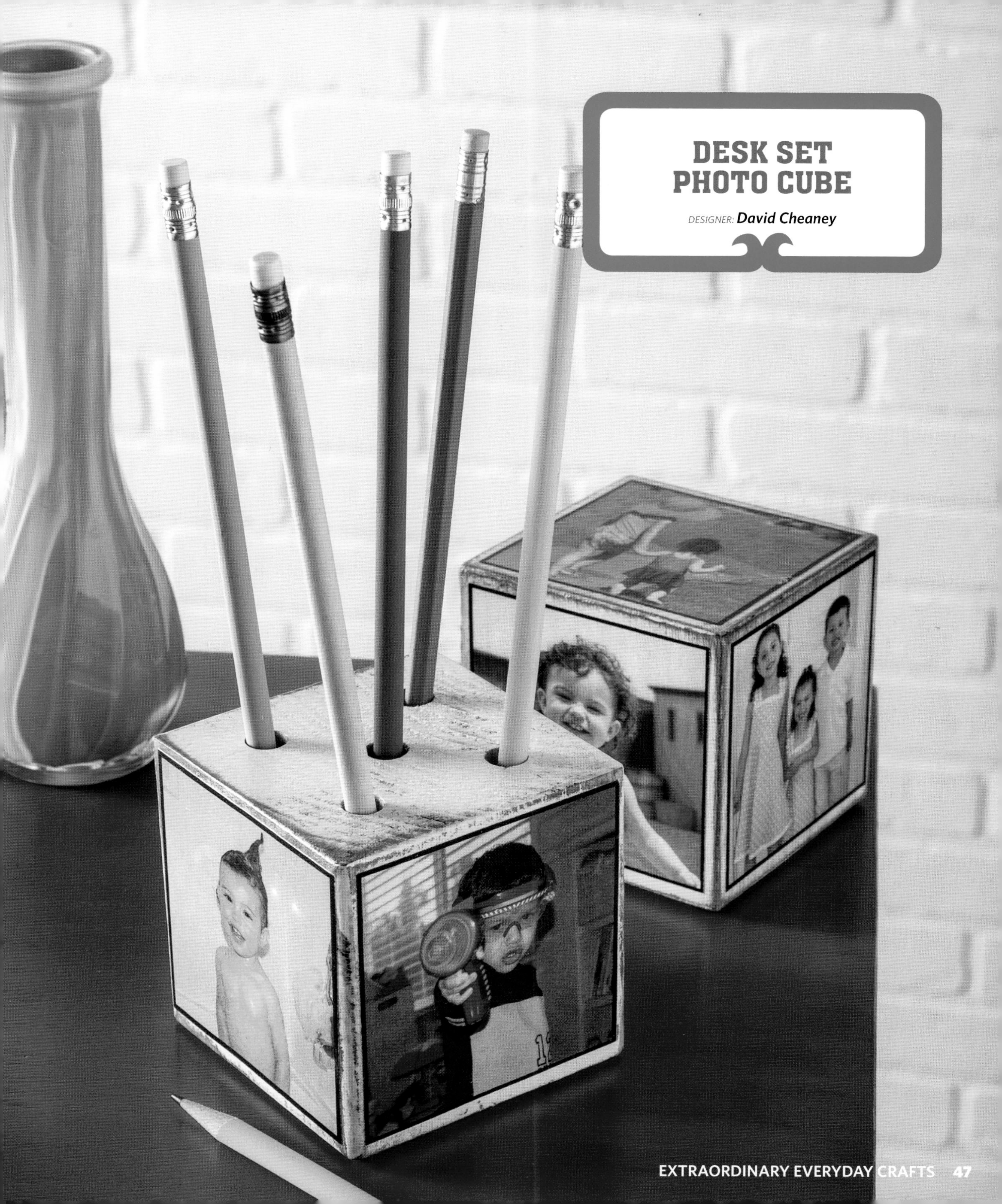

DESK SET PHOTO CUBE

Framed pictures are great desk decor, but sometimes there are space restraints, which require a creative solution. This desk set photo cube solves the problem— it's fun, functional, and easy to make!

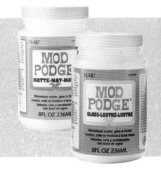

WHAT YOU'LL NEED   MOD PODGE MATTE   ■   MOD PODGE GLOSS   ■   FOLKART ACRYLIC PAINT, WICKER WHITE   ■   4 x 4-INCH (10 × 10 CM) WOOD BLOCK, CUT DOWN TO 3½ x 3½ INCH (8.9 x 8.9 CM)   ■   WOOD STAIN   ■   FOAM BRUSH RECOMMENDED   ■   SANDPAPER, #200 GRIT   ■   ELECTRIC DRILL   ■   ⁷⁄₁₆-INCH (1.1 CM) SPADE BIT (TO MAKE HOLES FOR PENCILS)   ■   PHOTOCOPIES SIZED 3 x 3 INCHES (7.6 x 7.6 CM) OR SIZE OF BLOCK   ■   SQUARE OF CORK OR FELT FOR THE BLOCK'S BOTTOM

WHAT YOU'LL DO

1   Stain edges only of the block and let dry.

2   Paint the entire block with FolkArt Acrylic Paint in Wicker White, including edges (A). Allow to dry.

3   When paint has dried, thoroughly sand the edges of the block, creating a distressed effect by removing some of the white paint (B). Experiment with different pressures while sanding to vary the look.

4   Use the cut side for the top of the block, leaving the smoother sides for the photos. To create holes for pens and pencils, mark the locations of the holes on the top face of the block and drill 1½-inch-deep (3.8 cm) holes with an electric drill and spade bit.

5   Working with one picture at a time, use a foam brush to apply Mod Podge Matte on the back of the picture and on a face of the block where a picture will go. Apply the picture and gently smooth out any bumps or air bubbles. Repeat the process on three more sides of the cube, and allow to dry.

6   Seal all the pictures with two coats of either Mod Podge Matte or Gloss, allowing the first coat to dry before applying the second.

7   Cut a piece of either cork or felt the size of the photo cube's bottom. Attach it with white craft glue (C), and let dry.

NO-SEW DECORATIVE PILLOWS

DESIGNER: ***Holli Nutter***

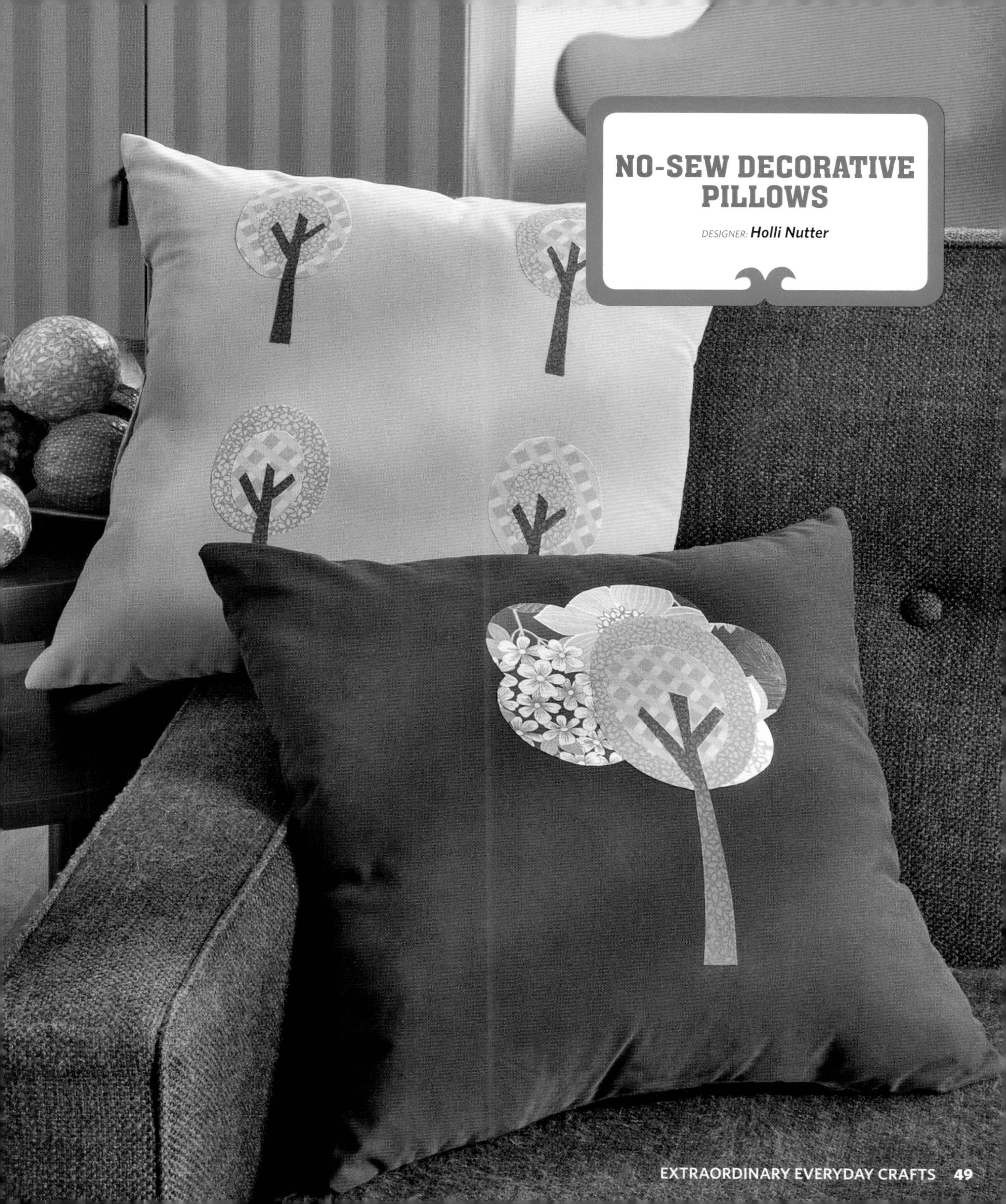

NO-SEW DECORATIVE PILLOWS

Who doesn't love resting on a beautiful decorative pillow? These are so easy to create and you don't even have to sew! With the help of Mod Podge Fabric, you can design your own decorative pillows to coordinate with every room in your home. These simple trees are perfect for beginners too.

WHAT YOU'LL NEED MOD PODGE BASIC TOOL KIT (PAGE 18) ■ MOD PODGE FABRIC ■ PREMADE THROW PILLOWS ■ DECORATIVE FABRICS (TWO TO THREE COORDINATING COLORS AND PATTERNS) ■ FABRIC SCISSORS ■ TRACING PAPER ■ MASKING TAPE OR STRAIGHT PINS ■ TEMPLATES (PAGE 233) ■ PENCIL

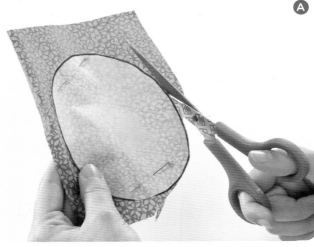

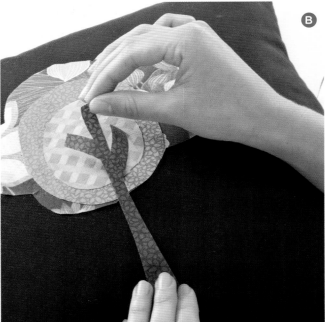

WHAT YOU'LL DO

1 Apply Mod Podge Fabric to the back side of the decorative fabrics to be appliquéd and allow to dry. This step will keep the fabric appliqués from fraying once cut.

2 Create a tracing-paper pattern for each appliqué section of the tree by tracing out the patterns provided in the Templates section of this book (page 233). Place each tracing paper pattern on the front or right side of the desired prepared fabric and either tape it in place or pin the pattern in place with straight pins. Cut out the fabric appliqués (A).

3 Next attach each fabric appliqué to the pillow front, working from the back layer of the design to the top layer of the large leaf shape before the smaller leaf shape, and lastly, add the tree trunk. For each appliqué, apply a coat of Mod Podge Fabric to the wrong side of the fabric appliqué, flip the appliqué over so the right side is facing out, and place appliqué layer on pillow where desired. Gently press to remove any captured air pockets, and smooth any wrinkles (B).

4 Repeat step 3 to continue attaching all appliqué designs to pillow, and allow to dry.

BONUS PROJECT

FABRIC-WRAPPED BALLS

A basket of decorated balls is a stylish statement to make in any home decor setting. When you create the decorative fabric-wrapped and decoupaged balls yourself, the results are very satisfying!

WHAT YOU'LL NEED MOD PODGE BASIC TOOL KIT (PAGE 18) ■ MOD PODGE FABRIC ■ 3-INCH (7.6 CM) STYROFOAM BALLS ■ ASSORTED FABRICS

WHAT YOU'LL DO

1 Apply Mod Podge Fabric to the wrong side of fabrics to be decoupaged. Let dry.

2 Measure and cut fabrics into ¾-inch-wide (19 mm) strips.

3 Attach fabric strips to Styrofoam balls using Mod Podge Fabric on the back of the strips. Press in place (A). Use several fabrics for variety.

4 Apply a topcoat of Mod Podge Fabric to each ball when fabric placement is complete. Let dry before using.

Ⓐ

CAN PLANTERS

DESIGNER: *Holli Nutter*

Recycling is good for the environment, and what better way to repurpose food cans than to make them pretty using decoupage techniques? These will look lovely outdoors on a back deck with either a potted plant or a candle or can be used indoors as shown in photo. Save your cans and create works of art; it is so much fun!

WHAT YOU'LL NEED MOD PODGE BASIC TOOL KIT (PAGE 18) ▪ MOD PODGE OUTDOOR ▪ MOD PODGE PODGEABLE CHIPBOARD SHAPES: DESIGNER ICONS ▪ FOLKART ACRYLIC PAINTS: LIME YELLOW, PURE ORANGE, MEDIUM ORANGE, TURQUOISE, ENGLISH MUSTARD ▪ 3 CLEAN RECYCLED FOOD CANS ▪ COORDINATING SCRAPBOOK PAPERS ▪ 12-GAUGE CRAFT WIRE ▪ SMALL WOODEN BEADS ▪ JUTE TWINE, NARROW ENOUGH TO FIT IN BEADS, A FEW YARDS OR METERS ▪ DRILL AND NARROW DRILL BIT, TO MAKE HOLES WIDE ENOUGH TO FIT WIRE ▪ RUBBING ALCOHOL ▪ PAPER TOWELS ▪ WIRE CUTTERS

WHAT YOU'LL DO

1 Check mouth of empty food cans for sharp edges, then wash in warm, soapy water. Rinse well and dry thoroughly. Wipe surface with a paper towel moistened with rubbing alcohol to remove any remaining grease or soap film.

2 Measure and cut scrapbook paper to fit height and circumference of recycled cans.

3 Glue scrapbook paper to cans using Mod Podge Outdoor on the cans and on the wrong side of the paper. Allow to dry. Once dry, brush a coat or two of Mod Podge Outdoor on the right side of the paper.

4 Paint wood beads using assorted FolkArt Acrylic Paint colors (listed above). Allow to dry.

5 To make handle, drill a small hole through side of each can, approximately ½ to 1 inch (1.2 to 2.5 cm) below rim. Repeat on opposite side of can.

6 Determine desired handle length and add a few inches; cut wire. Feed wire through one hole and secure by wrapping the end around itself. Thread painted beads onto wire; then slightly bend, creating handle. Insert second end into can, and secure it by wrapping the end onto itself (A).

7 Using a pencil, trace the Mod Podge Podgeable Chipboard Designer icon Butterly shape onto scrapbook paper and cut out paper. Apply paper to chipboard shape using Mod Podge Outdoor. Wrap butterfly's body area with jute twine and attach with Mod Podge Outdoor to the outside of the can.

8 Wrap jute twine as shown around cans. Secure ends with Mod Podge Outdoor.

9 String beads on jute twine, knotting twine between beads, and attach bead strings to cans as shown, using white craft glue. Let dry before using.

RECYCLED TEA LIGHT HOLDERS

DESIGNER: **Julie Lewis**

Turning the ordinary into the extraordinary with simple recycled food cans, decorative scrapbook papers, and candle holders.

WHAT YOU'LL NEED   MOD PODGE BASIC TOOL KIT (PAGE 18)   ⬚   MOD PODGE MATTE   ⬚   FOLKART HOME DÉCOR CHALK (IN COORDINATING COLORS)   ⬚   RECYCLED FOOD CANS, OR OTHER SHALLOW FOOD CANS, 3-OUNCE (85 G) SIZE   ⬚   RUBBING ALCOHOL   ⬚   COORDINATING SCRAPBOOK PAPERS   ⬚   GLASS OR WOODEN CANDLE HOLDERS, ONE FOR EACH CAN   ⬚   FINE-GRIT SANDPAPER   ⬚   MOD PODGE WONDER GLUE

WHAT YOU'LL DO

1 Wash empty food cans in warm soapy water. Rinse well and dry thoroughly. Wipe surface with a paper towel moistened with rubbing alcohol to remove any remaining grease or soap film.

2 Measure the depth of each tin can on the outside and cut a strip of scrapbook paper to fit around each can.

3 Brush Mod Podge Matte onto one section of can (A) and apply end of paper strip over it (B). Smooth paper around can as you continue to apply Mod Podge around the can. Repeat process for each can and let dry 20 minutes. Seal cans with additional coats of Mod Podge Matte, allowing to dry between coats.

4 Paint glass or wood candle holders with FolkArt Home Décor Chalk. Let dry. Lightly sand for a distressed look.

5 Turn decoupaged cans upside down and glue candle holders to can centers, using Mod Podge Wonder Glue. Let cure completely before using.

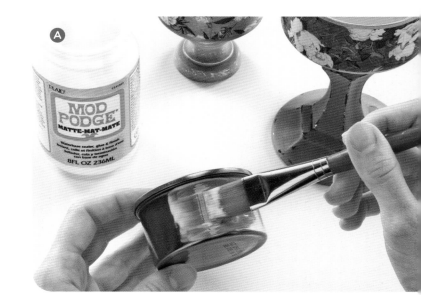

NAPKIN-COVERED GLASS VASES

DESIGNER: *Julie Lewis*

Taking plain glass vases to a highly decorative level is so easy with simple printed paper napkins and Mod Podge.

WHAT YOU'LL NEED   MOD PODGE DISHWASHER-SAFE, GLOSS   ▢   PRINTED PAPER NAPKINS WITH PRETTY DESIGN   ▢   ROUND AND SQUARE GLASS VASES   ▢   SCISSORS   ▢   FLAT BRUSH   ▢   RULER   ▢   PENCIL

WHAT YOU'LL DO

1   Separate printed napkins by peeling apart layers (A). Use different layers to create a bolder and more faded appearance.

NOTE: *You will be using the printed ply. The unprinted layers can be saved for other projects. For a delicate, more faded appearance, use only one layer. For a different look with a bolder appearance, use additional layers.*

2   For each vase, measure and cut the printed napkin to size, matching the height and circumference of the glass vase.

3   Working in sections, apply Mod Podge Dishwasher-Safe to glass surface. Next, place napkin over Mod Podge. Gently press in place, smoothing out any air bubbles and wrinkles. Use light pressure, to prevent napkin from tearing. Repeat until entire vase has been decoupaged. Allow to dry for 20 minutes.

4   Apply several coats of Mod Podge Dishwasher-Safe to seal paper napkin to surface (B). Allow to dry between each coat.

CANVAS WALL ART

DESIGNER: **Maggie Brereton**

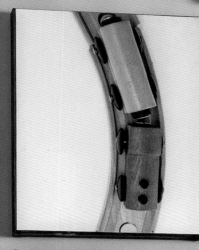

Create your very own personalized canvas wall art easily and inexpensively so you can showcase your family photographs or pictures of meaningful and well-loved items throughout your home, all without breaking the bank

WHAT YOU'LL NEED MOD PODGE GLOSS ▢ FOLKART ACRYLIC PAINT (COLOR OF CHOICE) ▢ 8 x 10-INCH (20.3 x 25 CM) WHITE STRETCHED CANVAS ▢ ½-INCH (13 MM) PAINTBRUSH ▢ 8 x 10-INCH (20.3 x 25 CM) PHOTOCOPIES OF PHOTOGRAPHS ▢ PAPER CUTTER OR SCISSORS

WHAT YOU'LL DO

1 Paint the edges and a small border on the front of each canvas with FolkArt Acrylic Paint (A). Let dry.

2 Trim each photograph with a paper cutter or scissors so that it fits nicely on the front of each canvas panel.

3 Working one canvas at a time, apply a thin coat of Mod Podge Gloss on the back of each photocopy, as well as on the front of each canvas. Position each photocopy on the canvas, making sure to smooth out any air bubbles, working from the center out. Let dry for 15–20 minutes.

4 To seal each photocopy, apply two more thin coats of Mod Podge Gloss, using nice long strokes and waiting 15–20 minutes between each coat. Let dry before hanging.

FAMILY MOD PODGE

Hands-on family activities, crafts for kids, plus quick
and easy ideas for children's room decor.

THE BIG

BOOK OF

MOD PODGE®

DECOUPAGED JOURNALS, PENCILS, AND UPCYCLED PENCIL CADDY

DESIGNER: **Chris Williams**

DECOUPAGED JOURNALS, PENCILS, AND UPCYCLED PENCIL CADDY

Whether you are going to school or working in an office, having a place to organize your lists is essential. Using a few scraps of paper, ribbon, embellishments, and a little Mod Podge, you can create a fun decoupaged journal, making it a special place to write down your thoughts, project lists, and schedules. Make it as simple or as decorated as you want, with layers or patchwork sections. Create extras for your friends. An accompanying pencil caddy and decoupaged pencils carry out the theme.

WHAT YOU'LL NEED MOD PODGE BASIC TOOL KIT (PAGE 18) ▢ MOD PODGE MATTE ▢ MOD PODGE MOD MELTS, MILK GLASS WHITE ▢ MOD PODGE MOD MOLDS: NATURE (BUTTERFLY), ROYAL ICONS (HEART), FLOWERS (ROSE AND LEAF) ▢ FOLKART MULTI-SURFACE PAINTS: MAGENTA AND TEAL, OR COLORS OF YOUR CHOICE ▢ 7-INCH (17.8 CM) CIRCULAR WOOD PLAQUE ▢ OATS CANISTER ▢ 3 COMPOSITION BOOKS ▢ NEW PENCILS ▢ ASSORTED SCRAPBOOK PAPERS ▢ ¾-INCH (19 MM) FLAT BRUSH ▢ HOT GLUE OR WHITE GLUE ▢ FLAT-BACK GEMS ▢ TEAL ORGANZA RIBBON ▢ GREEN RICKRACK ▢ MOD PODGE MOD MELTER ▢ MOD PODGE WONDER GLUE

WHAT YOU'LL DO

COMPOSITION BOOKS

1. Cut scrapbook papers as desired to cover the front, or both front and back, of each composition book. Play with your design, using a variety of colors or patterns of coordinating scrapbook papers. You can even use a photocopy of your favorite photograph to personalize your journal.

2. For each book, brush Mod Podge Matte onto the wrong side of each paper section to be decoupaged, and apply the sections one by one to the composition book, following the design you planned. Continue adding the scrapbook papers until all are decoupaged in place. Allow to dry.

3. The woven binding of each composition book can be painted a color that will match or coordinate with the paper design. Use a flat brush to paint the woven binding.

4. When journal covers are dry, apply one or two coats of Mod Podge Matte to the covers to seal and protect.

5. Embellishments of ribbons or rickrack only add to the charm. With Mod Podge Mod Molds, Mod Podge Mod Melts, and the Mod Podge Mod Melter, you can create, paint, and then adhere butterflies, hearts, and flowers (A). Either hot glue or white craft glue can be used to attach the embellishments to the journals.

PENCIL CADDY

1 Upcycling an empty oats canister into a pencil caddy is not only thrifty but also fun! Determine desired height of the pencil caddy; using a ruler, measure and mark around the canister.

2 Cut along marked line to create an open canister.

3 Cut patterned scrapbook paper to fit exterior of canister. Mod Podge the cut scrapbook paper to canister. Allow to dry. Brush a coat of Mod Podge Matte over exterior. Allow to dry.

4 Cut additional paper designs from scrapbook papers such as flowers and labels. Mod Podge these additional embellishments to the canister. Allow to dry.

5 Paint the interior of the canister with FolkArt Multi-Surface Paint in Teal. Allow to dry, and reapply paint, if necessary, to make it opaque.

6 Paint the routed edge of the small, round plaque using FolkArt Multi-Surface Paint in Teal. Allow to dry, and reapply paint, if necessary, to make it opaque. Allow to dry.

7 Cut patterned scrapbook paper in a circle to fit the top of the plaque. Mod Podge in place and allow to dry. Apply a topcoat of Mod Podge Matte to seal and protect.

8 When it is thoroughly dry, attach decorated canister to round plaque using Mod Podge Wonder Glue. Allow to dry.

9 Embellish completed pencil caddy with Mod Podge Mod Mold embellishments and/or ribbon, if desired.

PENCILS

1 Paint pencils using FolkArt Multi-Surface Paint in Teal, and allow to dry.

2 If desired, cut small strips of scrapbook paper and Mod Podge to Teal pencil in a spiraled manner.

3 Create Mod Podge Mod Melt hearts (one for each pencil). Paint hearts using FolkArt Multi-Surface Paint in Magenta, and allow to dry.

4 Adhere heart embellishments to metal rim of pencil using hot glue.

DOTS-AND-STRIPES BUTTON FRAME

DESIGNER: **Holli Nutter**

A photo frame is a perfect beginner project; it is simple to create and fun to display. A perfect duo!

WHAT YOU'LL NEED MOD PODGE BASIC TOOL KIT (PAGE 18) ■ MOD PODGE WASH OUT FOR KIDS ■ FOLKART ACRYLIC PAINT: WICKER WHITE ■ WOOD PICTURE FRAME OR MIRROR FRAME ■ YELLOW- STRIPED SCRAPBOOK PAPER ■ BRIGHTLY COLORED ASSORTED BUTTONS ■ WHITE CRAFT GLUE

WHAT YOU'LL DO

1 Paint wood frame using FolkArt Acrylic Paint in Wicker White. Let dry. Reapply basecoat, if desired.

2 Position frame, right-side down, onto the back of the striped paper, and trace frame shape with a pencil. Be sure stripes are parallel to the edges of the frame.

3 Cut paper along pencil lines.

4 Apply a thin coat of Mod Podge Wash Out for Kids to front of frame. Also apply Mod Podge Wash Out for Kids to the back of the paper, and position it carefully on the frame. Smooth paper with fingers from the center toward the outer edges. This will remove air bubbles and will smooth wrinkles. Allow to dry 15–20 minutes.

5 Apply a light coat of Mod Podge Wash Out for Kids all over the paper to seal it. Let dry.

6 Attach buttons to the frame with white craft glue (A). Let dry before using.

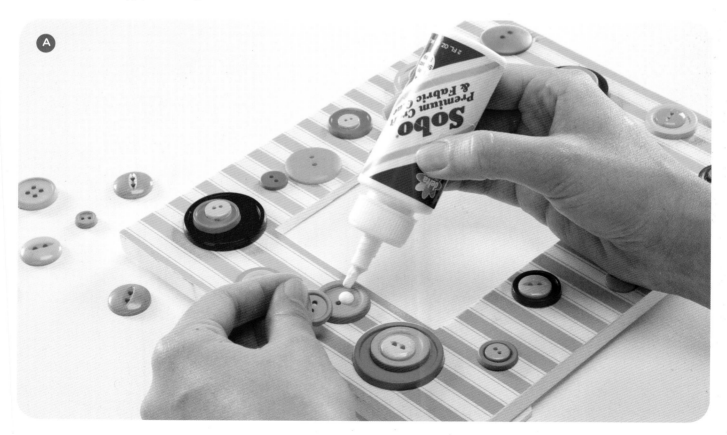

TILE DRINK COASTERS

DESIGNER: **Maggie Brereton**

Tile coasters make great personalized gifts for housewarmings, birthday gifts, and Christmas. Use pretty scrapbook paper or your favorite photocopies of photos to make these unique, one-of-a-kind coasters to brighten up any room in the house.

WHAT YOU'LL NEED   MOD PODGE BASIC TOOL KIT (PAGE 18)   ☐   MOD PODGE FURNITURE MATTE   ☐
WHITE CRAFT GLUE   ☐   4¼ x 4¼-INCH (10.8 x 10.8 CM) SQUARE WHITE CERAMIC TILES   ☐   4 x 4-INCH
(10 x 10 CM) SCRAPBOOK PAPER SQUARES OR PHOTOCOPIES OF PHOTOGRAPHS (ONE FOR EACH TILE)   ☐
4 x 4-INCH (10 x 10 CM) FELT SQUARES (ONE FOR EACH TILE)

WHAT YOU'LL DO

1   With a ¾-inch (19 mm) flat brush, apply one thin coat of Mod Podge Furniture Matte to the top, or shiny side, of each ceramic tile. Also apply one thin coat of Mod Podge Furniture Matte to wrong side of paper squares.

2   Position one square of scrapbook paper or a photograph photocopy over the top of the Mod Podge-covered ceramic tile, and smooth out any air bubbles, working from the center out. Let dry for 2 hours.

3   To seal scrapbook paper or photographs onto tiles, apply two or three thin coats of Mod Podge Furniture Matte over top with a paintbrush (A). Allow drying time of 1 hour between coats.

4   Let the coasters dry for 4 weeks, which enables Mod Podge Furniture Matte to completely cure. Once cured, surface may be used as a drink holder and then cleaned with a damp cloth.

5   Attach a felt square to the bottom of each tile coaster with white craft glue or hot glue. This will help to protect furniture surfaces. Let dry before using.

SAFARI ANIMAL BIRTHDAY PARTY

DESIGNER: **Rachel Faucett**

Children's birthday parties are so much fun, and when you create a themed party, complete with invitations, signs or banners and party hats, the birthday child feels so special!

WHAT YOU'LL NEED   MOD PODGE BASIC TOOL KIT (PAGE 18)   ☐   MOD PODGE PAPER, MATTE OR GLOSS   ☐
MOD PODGE MOD MELT, NEON   ☐   MOD PODGE MOD MOLD, CELEBRATION   ☐   FOLKART MULTI-SURFACE
PAINT, METALLIC BRIGHT GOLD   ☐   SMALL DETAIL PAINT BRUSH   ☐   BRIGHTLY COLORED CARDSTOCK:
ORANGE, BLUE, YELLOW   ☐   DIGITAL IMAGES OF SAFARI ANIMALS   ☐   WHITE COPY PAPER   ☐   MOD PODGE
MOD MELTER   ☐   ALPHABET STAMP SET   ☐   STAMP PAD, BLACK   ☐   ⅛-INCH DIAMETER (3.2 MM) WOOD
DOWEL RODS (ONE FOR EACH SIGN)   ☐   WHITE CRAFT GLUE   ☐   TRACING PAPER   ☐   TEMPLATE (PAGE 231)

WHAT YOU'LL DO

PARTY INVITATIONS

1. Fold brightly colored cardstock in half to create a note. Cardstock can be folded either horizontally or vertically, depending on size and shape of safari animal. Be sure notes will fit in envelopes for invitations. Set notes aside.

2. Print safari animal images found on Internet onto white copy paper sized to fit the front half of the cardstock notes. Using scissors, trim around each animal, leaving a ⅛-inch (3.2 mm) halo.

3. Using Mod Podge Paper, decoupage each safari animal print onto another piece of brightly colored cardstock. Allow to dry.

4. Trim colored cardstock around animal shape, allowing ¼-inch (6 mm) halo around animal shape.

5. Adhere the colored cardstock with animal cutout onto front of folded card using Mod Podge Paper. Allow to dry. Do this for all the animal cutouts.

6. Stamp a message such as PARTY TIME or LET'S PARTY or YOU'RE INVITED TO A WILD PARTY onto cardstock.

7. Create several birthday party–hat shape and pennant-shape Mod Podge Mod Mold embellishments using the Mod Podge Neon Mod Melts and the Mod Podge Celebration Mod Mold. To do this, insert a Mod Podge Mod Melt into a Mod Podge Mod Melter. Allow to heat up. Fill the Mod Podge Celebration Mod Mold with the heated Mod Podge Mod Melt. Allow to cool; remove molded pieces from silicone mold.

8. Highlight the polka dots and trim on the molded birthday hat embellishments by painting them FolkArt Multi-Surface Paint in Metallic Bright Gold. Allow to dry. Attach Mod Podge Mod Mold embellishments to the safari animal heads using craft glue or Mod Podge Mod Melts. Attach a Mod Molded "necklace" of pennants around an animal's neck.

PARTY SIGNS

1. Cut dowels 12 inches (30.5 cm) in length, one for each sign.

2. Cut colored cardstock 4 x 6 inches (10 x 15.2 cm) in a variety of colors, one piece for each sign.

3. Print safari animals onto white copy paper sized slightly smaller than the cut colored cardstock.

4. Using Mod Podge Paper, adhere the printed safari animal onto the front of the colored cardstock. Allow to dry.

5. Stamp a message such as GO WILD or PARTY ANIMAL or ROAR onto the base of each cardstock sign.

6. Center the signs and attach them to the dowels using Mod Podge Mod Melts.

SAFARI ANIMAL BIRTHDAY PARTY

PARTY HATS

1 Trace the cone template for the party hats onto tracing paper (see the Templates section, page 231), cut out, and then trace onto colored cardstock. Trace out one cone for each hat. Cut out cone shapes but leave them flat for now.

2 For each hat, cut a 1½-inch tall (3.8 cm) strip of green cardstock that will be long enough to fit around the base of the party hat. Make narrowly spaced vertical cuts into the green cardstock strip to make fringe, creating clumps of grass.

3 For each hat, print a safari animal onto white copy paper, and size it to fit the height of the party hat. Trim around animal.

4 Using Mod Podge Paper, adhere animal to cardstock party hat (A). Allow to dry.

5 Add a few sprigs of paper grass to the top of the hat, attaching to the wrong side of the party hat. Allow to dry.

6 Curl the party hat into a cone shape, overlapping ends slightly. Glue in place using craft glue or Mod Podge Mod Melt.

7 Cut green cardstock grass into smaller strips, approximately 1 inch (2.5 cm) wide. Attach grass sections with Mod Podge Paper to base of party hat, overlapping sections following the curve of the hat (B).

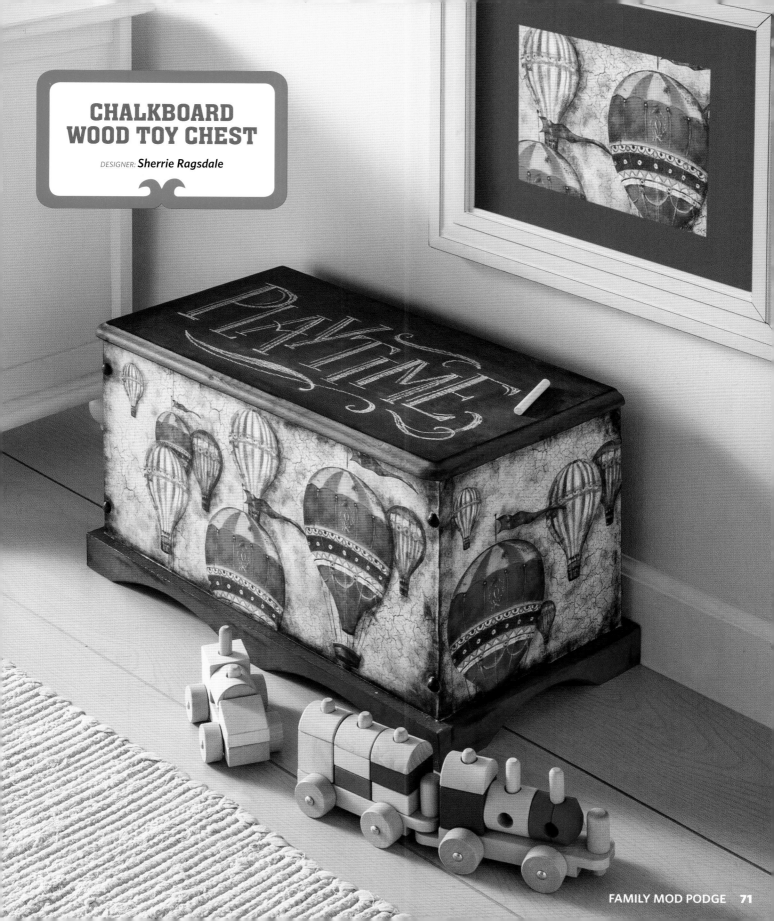

CHALKBOARD WOOD TOY CHEST

DESIGNER: **Sherrie Ragsdale**

CHALKBOARD WOOD TOY CHEST

Keeping track of toys or just making a daily statement is easier to do with a colorful toy chest and chalkboard lid.

WHAT YOU'LL NEED MOD PODGE BASIC TOOL KIT (PAGE 18) ■ MOD PODGE FURNITURE GLOSS ■
FOLKART ACRYLIC PAINTS: CARDINAL RED AND REAL BROWN ■ FOLKART CHALKBOARD PAINT, BLACK
■ WOOD TOY CHEST WITH LID ■ THREE PHOTOCOPIES OF POSTERS (REDUCED TO FIT TOY CHEST
FRONT AND TWO SIDES) ■ WHITE CHALK ■ MOD PODGE BRUSH APPLICATOR

WHAT YOU'LL DO

1 Apply a basecoat to the toy chest body and rim of lid, using FolkArt Acrylic Paint in Cardinal Red. Let dry and then dry brush FolkArt Acrylic Paint in Real Brown on top of those surfaces for an aged look.

2 Measure and cut photocopies of posters to fit front and two sides of toy chest.

3 Brush Mod Podge Furniture Gloss onto one side of chest to be decoupaged, and apply photocopy. Cover with waxed paper and smooth out bubbles with Mod Podge Squeegee, working from the center outward. Repeat process for front

and remaining side of chest. Let dry 20 minutes before applying several coats of Mod Podge Furniture Gloss (A) to seal and protect.

4 Using a large flat brush, apply black FolkArt Chalkboard to lid of toy chest. Allow to dry, and reapply one to two more additional coats. Let dry thoroughly.

5 Condition chalkboard by rubbing side of chalk over entire surface. Then wipe with paper towel before writing on it with chalk.

**MOD PODGE
GARDEN WAGON**

DESIGNER: **Sherrie Ragsdale**

MOD PODGE GARDEN WAGON

Make pretty garden flowers happy by placing them on a pretty little colored wagon.
For decorative use only.

WHAT YOU'LL NEED MOD PODGE BASIC TOOL KIT (PAGE 18) ▪ MOD PODGE OUTDOOR ▪ FOLKART MULTI-SURFACE PAINT: TEAL, WICKER WHITE, AND LICORICE ▪ OLD WAGON ▪ 12 x 12-INCH (30.5 x 30.5 CM) PIECES OF ASSORTED COLOR COORDINATING SCRAPBOOK PAPERS ▪ COARSE SANDPAPER ▪ CLOTH OR RAG FOR WIPING ▪ SPOOL OF TWINE FOR WRAPPING HANDLE ▪ METAL FLOWERS ▪ WIRE CUTTERS ▪ MOD PODGE WONDER GLUE

WHAT YOU'LL DO

1 Basecoat wagon with FolkArt Multi-Surface Paint in Teal. Allow to dry. Sand to distress. Wipe clean with rag.

2 Choose papers that coordinate with the base color. Measure the height of the wagon side and then cut strips of that height measurement by 12 inches (30.5 cm). Cut several strips, enough to wrap around the entire wagon.

3 Using Mod Podge Outdoor, apply the paper strips to the wagon. Allow to dry.

4 Apply Mod Podge Outdoor to the shaft of the handle and then wrap twine around it. Allow to dry.

5 Apply Mod Podge Outdoor to the entire wagon surface to seal and protect both the paper and twine. Allow to dry. Then reapply one to two additional applications of Mod Podge Outdoor, providing for drying time between applications.

6 Cut stems off the metal flowers, and paint flowers, using FolkArt Multi-Surface Paint in Licorice. Allow to dry.

7 Paint the flower centers with FolkArt Multi-Surface Paint in Wicker White. Let dry.

8 Glue metal flowers to the wagon wheels using Mod Podge Wonder Glue (A).

PLASTIC ELEPHANT BOOKENDS

DESIGNER: **Sherrie Ragsdale**

PLASTIC ELEPHANT BOOKENDS

Coming or going, this whimsical elephant bookend can bring bright color and a smile to anyone's face. Use another animal if you prefer, and adapt paint colors.

WHAT YOU'LL NEED   MOD PODGE BASIC TOOL KIT (PAGE 18)   ■   MOD PODGE MATTE   ■   FOLKART MULTI-SURFACE PAINTS: VIOLET PANSY AND AQUA   ■   LARGE PLASTIC TOY ANIMAL   ■   4 WOOD PLAQUES, EACH 5 x 6½ INCHES (12.7 x 16.5CM), OR EXISTING WOOD BOOKENDS   ■   COORDINATING SCRAPBOOK PAPERS   ■   COORDINATING FABRIC   ■   ASSORTED COLORED BUTTONS   ■   ¼-INCH-WIDE (6 MM) PURPLE SATIN RIBBON   ■   JIGSAW OR CRAFT KNIFE   ■   MOD PODGE WONDER GLUE

WHAT YOU'LL DO

1 Cut plastic elephant body in half. Depending on thickness of plastic, it can be cut using either a craft knife or a jigsaw. Paint both elephant sections with FolkArt Multi-Surface Paint in Violet Pansy and the tusks in Aqua. Allow to dry.

2 Glue two 5 x 6½-inch (12.7 x 16.5 cm) plaques together. Glue two more together to make the bookend pair. As an alternative solution, use a pair of existing wood bookends. Paint bookends with FolkArt Multi-Surface Paint in Violet Pansy.

3 Cut scrapbook paper to fit inside surfaces of bookends that will face the books. Working one bookend at a time, brush Mod Podge Matte onto surfaces as well as wrong side of paper. Cover with waxed paper and smooth with Mod Podge Squeegee. Repeat process with paper on the outside surface of bookends, which will face the animal, using a coordinating paper. When dry, cover papers with a layer of Mod Podge Matte (A).

4 Using Mod Podge Wonder Glue, glue one cut end of elephant to outer vertical section of bookend. Do the same for the second half of the elephant.

5 Brush Mod Podge onto fabric until thoroughly saturated. Let dry.

6 Cut two half circles from fabric, large enough to create a blanket on the elephant's back. Using Mod Podge Matte, attach fabric half circle to back of animal on each bookend.

7 Embellish fabric blanket by gluing on assorted colored buttons. Glue a strip of purple satin ribbon around elephant to cover where cut end is glued to bookend.

MINATURE TOY CAR STORAGE TIN

DESIGNER: *Walter Silva*

MINIATURE TOY CAR STORAGE TIN

This storage container for those lightning-fast cars is super-easy and quick to make!

WHAT YOU'LL NEED MOD PODGE BASIC TOOL KIT (PAGE 18) ☐ MOD PODGE HARD COAT ☐ NEWSPAPER ☐ RECYCLED COOKIE TIN ☐ DIE CUTTING MACHINE ☐ COLORING BOOK IMAGES OF RACE CARS ☐ MINIATURE TOY CAR ☐ ¾-INCH (1.9 CM) DIAMETER MAGNET ☐ MOD PODGE WONDER GLUE

WHAT YOU'LL DO

1 Cut newspaper into sections. Decoupage onto the sides and top of cookie tin, using Mod Podge Hard Coat (A).

2 Using coloring book race-car images, decoupage one racing car image on each side of the cookie tin.

3 Create a racetrack out of scrapbook paper, and decoupage to the center of the tin's lid.

4 Using a die cutting machine, create die-cut letters to spell SPEED and TURBO. Decoupage the words, one letter at a time, on the lid.

5 Seal the whole tin with Mod Podge Hard Coat.

6 Attach a ¾-inch (1.9 cm) round magnet to the bottom of the miniature toy car with Mod Podge Wonder Glue. Place on top of the lid. This will secure the car to the tin lid.

PARTY BEVERAGE BUCKET

DESIGNER: *Walter Silva*

PARTY BEVERAGE BUCKET

Overlapping geometric triangle patterns create a kaleidoscope of color on this party beverage bucket.

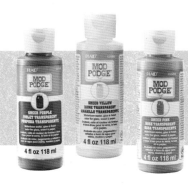

WHAT YOU'LL NEED MOD PODGE SHEER COLORS: PINK, PURPLE, AND YELLOW ▢ MOD PODGE BASIC SHAPES TRACING TEMPLATE ▢ MOD PODGE SPOUNCER SET ▢ 7.2 QUART (6.8 L) PLASTIC STORAGE BIN, WITH LID ▢ 3 DISPOSABLE FOAM PLATES

WHAT YOU'LL DO

1 Put a small puddle of Mod Podge Sheer Color Yellow on a foam plate. Load a Mod Podge Spouncer with Yellow by dabbing it into the puddle. Using the tall triangle tracing template as a stencil, spounce two yellow triangles to both long sides of the storage bin (see photo for reference). Add one yellow triangle to the ends of the storage bin that have the handles. Let dry. Clean spouncer, and wipe template to remove excess Mod Podge Sheer Color.

2 Add a small puddle of Mod Podge Sheer Color Purple to a foam plate. Invert triangle template and apply three purple triangles to long sides of the bin. Add two purple triangles on each short end of the bin also. Let dry. Clean spouncer and template.

3 Add a small puddle of Mod Podge Sheer Color Pink to a foam plate. Load a spouncer with Pink. For the long sides of the bin, spounce three triangles with the pink, slightly lower than the top yellow triangles (A). Next, invert triangle template and spounce two pink triangles, slightly lower than the purple triangles. Spounce two pink triangles for the short sides of the bin and add one inverted pink triangle at the bottom of those sides. Let dry.

4 Fill interior with ice, and add an assortment of your favorite beverages.

A

TOTALLY TWEENS

Here are some fun ideas for tweens to personalize their world.

THE BIG

BOOK OF MOD PODGE®

GLITTERED AND TINTED GLASS JARS

DESIGNER: *Amy Anderson*

Decorating with glass jars and bottles is even more fun now, using Mod Podge Sheer Colors and Mod Podge Podgeable Glitters.

WHAT YOU'LL NEED MOD PODGE SHEER COLORS (COLORS OF CHOICE) ▪ MOD PODGE ROCKS! PEEL & STICK STENCILS: DOT PATTERN, WOOD GRAIN, AND SKELETON KEYS ▪ MOD PODGE GLOSS ▪ MASON JARS AND/OR RECYCLED GLASS BOTTLES ▪ CHIPBOARD SHAPES ▪ FOLKART ACRYLIC PAINT: COLORS OF YOUR CHOICE ▪ MOD PODGE SPOUNCERS ▪ MOD PODGE PODGEABLE GLITTERS ▪ BAKER'S TWINE ▪ SCISSORS ▪ PAINTBRUSH ▪ RUBBING ALCOHOL ▪ LARGE PAPER CUPS, ONE FOR EACH JAR

WHAT YOU'LL DO

1 Clean and dry jars. Swirl rubbing alcohol on the inside to remove any leftover residue, and let dry.

2 For each jar, pour Mod Podge Sheer Color (in your desired color) into a jar. Begin by adding two to three tablespoons and swirl around the inside until it covers the entire jar. If needed, add a small amount of Mod Podge Sheer Colors at a time. Turn the jar upside down over a paper cup and let the excess drain out. Allow to sit for a couple of hours. Then turn right-side up and let dry until the color is completely transparent.

3 While jars are drying, paint desired chipboard shapes with acrylic paint on both sides and let dry.

4 Remove Mod Podge Rocks! Peel & Stick Stencil from the backer sheet and place onto the front of the jar, centering the design. Smooth with your fingers.

5 Use a Mod Podge Spouncer to apply Mod Podge Gloss through the stencil design (A). Remove the stencil immediately.

6 Sprinkle Mod Podge Podgeable Glitter on top of the wet Mod Podge design (B) and let dry. While your glitter design is drying, wash the stencil and return it to the backer.

7 Repeat steps 4–6 above on the other jars, and/or add stenciled designs to the chipboard shapes.

8 Let everything dry; then cut a length of baker's twine and tie a chipboard shape around the mouth of a jar (C).

FAUX CUPCAKE
PHOTO HOLDERS

DESIGNER: *Andrea Currie*

Celebrate a special occasion with a super-sweet cupcake photo holder. Just don't forget: it's not real!

WHAT YOU'LL NEED   MOD PODGE GLOSS ☐   MOD PODGE COLLAGE CLAY, VANILLA WHITE ☐   MOD PODGE MOD MELTS (IN VARIOUS COLORS) ☐   3-INCH (7.6 CM) FOAM BALLS, ONE FOR EACH CUPCAKE ☐   GLITTER: BROWN AND WHITE ☐   FOAM BRUSH ☐   JUMBO CUPCAKE LINERS, ONE FOR EACH CUPCAKE ☐   LARGE WASHERS OR (SOMETHING FLAT AND HEAVY FOR STABILITY), ONE FOR EACH CUPCAKE ☐   BOBBY PINS ☐   SMALL RHINESTONES ☐   GLASS BEAD GLITTER (OPTIONAL) ☐   QUICK-DRYING MULTIPURPOSE GLUE ☐   PARCHMENT PAPER ☐ MOD PODGE MOD MELTER ☐   MOD PODGE WONDER GLUE

WHAT YOU'LL DO

1 Flatten the foam ball on one side by pressing onto a hard surface.

2 Push bobby pin about ½-inch (1.2 cm) into the rounded top of the foam ball, with curved side of pin in; pull it out and glue it back with dab of Mod Podge Mod Melt or hot glue.

3 Dab a generous amount of Mod Podge Gloss all the way around the lower "cake" portion of the foam ball, using a foam brush. Quickly sprinkle brown glitter over Mod Podge Gloss (A). Repeat if necessary.

4 Add a washer to the bottom of the cupcake liner (B), and add hot glue or Mod Podge Mod Melts on top of washer. Quickly press the foam ball into the cupcake liner.

FAUX CUPCAKE PHOTO HOLDERS

5 Starting about ½-inch (1.3 cm) up from the cupcake liner, pipe Mod Podge Collage Clay Vanilla White around the foam ball, just as you would with a real cupcake (C). Sprinkle white glitter while Mod Podge Collage Clay is still moist.

6 Insert colored Mod Podge Mod Melt into the Mod Podge Mod Melter. When Mod Podge Collage Clay Vanilla White is fully dry, pipe on Mod Podge Mod Melt "syrup" (in color of your choice). Sprinkle glitter or glass beads while the Mod Podge Mod Melt "frosting" is still warm (D).

7 Add larger embellishments such as rhinestones and Mod Podge Mod Melt charms with Mod Podge Wonder Glue (E). Adhere embellishments to bobby pin by first placing a piece of parchment paper inside the pin to keep the excess glue from sealing both parts of the pin together.

PAPER DOT BEADS

DESIGNER: **Candie Cooper**

PAPER DOT BEADS

Jewelry making has always been a love of mine, but how cool is it to say you actually created the bead too! Mod Podge paper beads are fun to create for jewelry crafters of all ages.

WHAT YOU'LL NEED MOD PODGE HARD COAT ☐ HEAVY MAGAZINE PAPERS, ASSORTED COLORS ☐ 1-HOLE PUNCH ☐ SMALL FLAT PAINTBRUSH ☐ 5 WOODEN MACRAMÉ BEADS, 1-INCH (2.5 CM) DIAMETER, AND 4 BARREL-SHAPED WOODEN BEADS ☐ 6 LARGE-HOLED SILVER SPACER BEADS ☐ ½-INCH-WIDE (1.3 CM) SATIN RIBBON, 3 FEET (91 CM), IN COLOR OF YOUR CHOICE ☐ PAPER PLATE ☐ SKEWER OR PAINTBRUSH (OPTIONAL)

WHAT YOU'LL DO

1 Punch holes out of magazine papers and lay punched circles out on a paper plate.

2 Slide the bead onto the end of a skewer or paintbrush. Paint a layer of Mod Podge Hard Coat onto the wood bead, around the holes.

3 Pick up the paper dots with the paintbrush and lay them around the holes of a round bead; press in place. Seal with Mod Podge Hard Coat, and start a second row by placing a paper dot slightly below the beginning of the first paper dot (approximately three-fourths down) to create an overlapping pattern like fish scales (A).

4 Cover the entire bead with paper dot "scales," sealing each row with Mod Podge Hard Coat as you go.

5 Set the bead aside while it dries, and start a new bead. Repeat for a total of five round beads.

6 Seal all the beads with a second coat of Mod Podge Hard Coat to create a really shiny surface.

7 Leaving a foot of ribbon before the knot, tie a knot in the ribbon and string a silver spacer bead onto the ribbon, followed by a paper dot bead. Continue in this alternating bead pattern for the remaining beads (B).

8 After you add all the necessary beads, tie a finishing knot next to the last bead to secure the beads in place.

9 Trim the tails of ribbon at an angle and seal the cut edge with Mod Podge Hard Coat to prevent fraying.

10 Tie the necklace around your neck and secure with a bow.

(A)

(B)

REPURPOSED COMPACT

DESIGNER: **Carol Cook**

REPURPOSED COMPACT

Transform a used makeup compact into an altered piece of art that serves a purpose. Use as a trinket box to carry small items such as jewelry or a travel sewing kit. Practical can also be fun and beautiful!

WHAT YOU'LL NEED   MOD PODGE BASIC TOOL KIT (PAGE 18)   ▪   MOD PODGE MATTE   ▪   MOD PODGE MOD MELT, METALLIC GOLD   ▪   MOD PODGE MOD MOLD, TRAVEL   ▪   MOD PODGE WONDER GLUE   ▪   FOLKART ACRYLIC PAINT, GOLD   ▪   EMPTY POWDER COMPACT   ▪   12 x 12-INCH (30.5 x 30.5 CM) SHEET OF SCRAPBOOK PAPER   ▪   SCRAPS OF PRINTED TISSUE PAPER   ▪   PERMANENT STAMPING INK   ▪   SELF-ADHESIVE RHINESTONES (IN GRADUATING SIZES; BLACK IN MODEL)   ▪   PAPER FLOWERS (BLACK IN MODEL)   ▪   MOD PODGE MOD MELTER

WHAT YOU'LL DO

1   Remove makeup pan from compact. Wash thoroughly and dry.

2   Using the compact as a guide, trace and cut out three circles, from scrapbook paper (A).

3   Tear around the edges of each circle, a bit, so it doesn't look round (B).

4   Adhere paper circles to compact top, bottom, and inside. Working with one circle at a time, brush a coat of Mod Podge Matte on the compact surface; brush a second coat of Mod Podge Matte onto the back of the paper. Press paper in place to remove air bubbles or wrinkles, working from the center outward.

5   Tear small scraps of tissue paper and apply them randomly to the compact top with Mod Podge Matte.

6   Create the Eiffel Tower embellishment from the Mod Podge Travel Mod Mold, using the Mod Podge Metallic Gold Mod Melt. Cover lightly with FolkArt Acrylic Paint in Gold and then lightly with stamping ink.

7   Glue Mod Podge Eiffel Tower Mod Mold embellishment to the top of the compact.

8   Glue paper flowers to the top of the compact using Mod Podge Wonder Glue.

9   Apply self-adhesive rhinestones to the top of the compact, following the shape of the circle, starting with the largest and ending with the smallest (see photo).

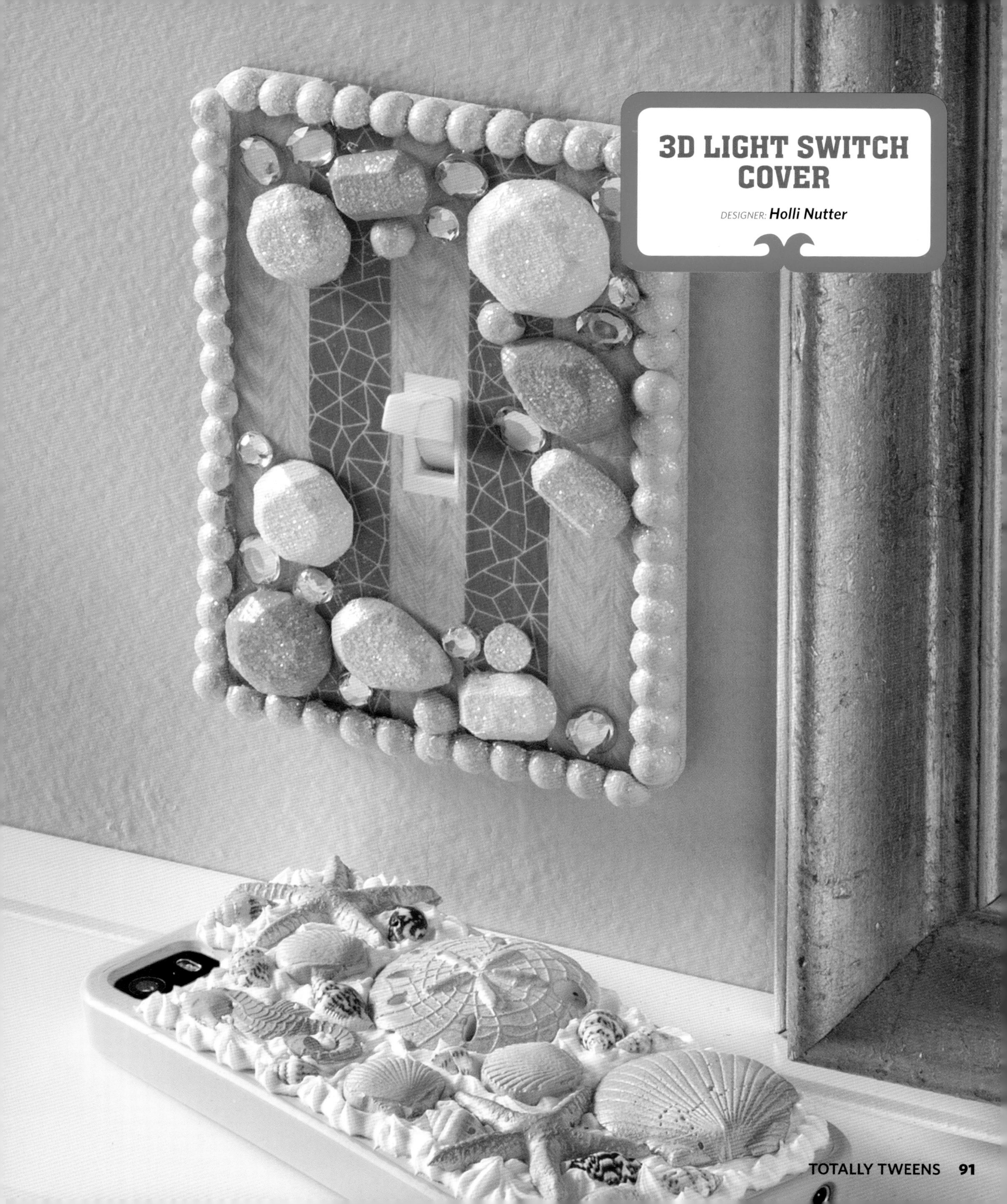

3D LIGHT SWITCH COVER

DESIGNER: ***Holli Nutter***

3D LIGHT SWITCH COVER

Who says all artwork should be in a frame? Have you considered decorating a light switch plate? Here's a nifty idea, and it's so easy and fun!

WHAT YOU'LL NEED MOD PODGE BASIC TOOL KIT (PAGE 18) ■ LIGHT SWITCH PLATE ■ MOD PODGE MOD MELT, MILK GLASS WHITE ■ MOD PODGE MOD MOLD, GEMS ■ MOD PODGE MATTE ■ FOLKART ACRYLIC COLORS: BRIGHT BABY PINK, JAMAICAN SEA, CALYPSO SKY, AND SHEER BLOSSOM ■ SMALL FLAT PAINTBRUSH ■ 2 WASHI TAPES, COORDINATING COLORS ■ CRYSTAL GLITTER ■ ASSORTED SHINY FLAT-BACK GEMS ■ MOD PODGE MOD MELTER ■ WHITE CRAFT GLUE

WHAT YOU'LL DO

1 Paint the light switch cover using FolkArt Acrylic Paint in Jamaican Sea. When it is dry, apply a light coat of Mod Podge Matte. When the Mod Podge Matte is dry, apply washi tape symmetrically on cover. Cut out center switch hole and screw holes from tape with craft knife.

2 Create several gems in a variety of sizes using Mod Podge Mod Melts, Mod Podge Gems Mod Mold, and the Mod Podge Mod Melter. Also make six strings of the pearl border in the Mod Mold.

3 Paint gems and pearls using coordinating colors listed above (A).

4 Apply a light coat of Mod Podge Matte to each gem and to the pearl border. Then sprinkle with crystal glitter (B).

5 Attach gems and borders as shown in photo, using white craft glue. Let dry before use.

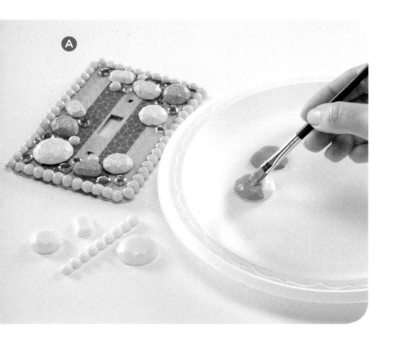

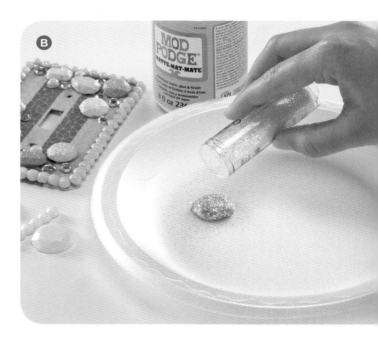

BONUS PROJECT

3D PHONE COVER

Want to make a fashion statement with your cell phone? Decorate your phone case in the Decoden style using Mod Podge Collage Clay. Take it a step further and create your own embellishments using Mod Podge Mod Melts and Mod Molds!

WHAT YOU'LL NEED   MOD PODGE MOD MELTER   ■   MOD POGE MOD MELT, MILK GLASS WHITE   ■   MOD PODGE MOD MOLD, SEA LIFE   ■   MOD PODGE COLLAGE CLAY, VANILLA WHITE, WITH STAR TIP   ■   FOLKART ACRYLIC PAINTS: JAMAICAN SEA, PARCHMENT, PARISIAN PINK, GILDED OAK, AND SUMMER PEACH   ■   CELL PHONE CASE   ■   SMALL FLAT BRUSH   ■   SMALL STENCIL BRUSH   ■   SHELL BEADS

WHAT YOU'LL DO

1 To create several Sea Life embellishments, insert Mod Podge Mod Melt into Mod Podge Mod Melter. When it is heated, squeeze melt into Mod Podge Sea Life Mod Mold to create one sand dollar, two starfish, one seahorse, one large scallop, and three small scallops.

2 Paint the embellishments with FolkArt Acrylic Paints. Color the starfish and sand dollar Parchment. Use Parisian Pink for the large scallop. Paint the seahorse Summer Peach. Apply Jamaican Sea to the small scallops.

3 Use the stencil brush to drybrush painted shells with contrasting colors to bring out the details in the designs.

4 Attach the star tip to the Mod Podge Collage Clay piping bag, and apply Mod Podge Collage Clay Vanilla White to the back of the phone case in small connected stars.

5 Carefully place painted embellishments into wet Mod Podge Collage Clay Vanilla White. Fill blank areas with shell beads.

6 Allow project to cure 1–5 days before using it.

LOVE WOOD LETTERS

DESIGNER: **Holli Nutter**

LOVE is in the air, or is it on the wall? Have fun creating these collaged letters and you too will enjoy LOVE in your life!

WHAT YOU'LL NEED MOD PODGE BASIC TOOL KIT (PAGE 18) ☐ MOD PODGE MATTE ☐ MOD PODGE DIMENSIONAL MAGIC, CLEAR ☐ MOD PODGE PODGEABLE PAPERS, ANTIQUE URBAN ☐ MOD PODGE PODGEABLE METAL BLANKS ☐ PAPERS WITH INSPIRING WORDS TO FIT MOD PODGE PODGEABLE METAL BLANKS ☐ FOLKART ACRYLIC PAINT, TEAL AND SEAMIST ☐ WOOD LETTERS L, O, V, AND E (YOUR CHOICE OF SIZE) ☐ COORDINATING SCRAPBOOK PAPERS ☐ LARGE FLAT BRUSH FOR PAINTING ☐ PARAFFIN WAX ☐ 4 PAPER FLOWERS ☐ MOD PODGE MOD MELTER ☐ MOD PODGE CLEAR MOD MELTS

WHAT YOU'LL DO

1 Paint wood letters with FolkArt Acrylic Paint in Teal and allow them to dry. When they are dry, rub paraffin wax on the edges of each letter. Paint over letters and paraffin wax with FolkArt Acrylic Paint in Seamist. Let dry.

2 Lightly sand letters to distress until some of the darker shade of paint shows through on the edges.

3 Flip letters over right-side down and trace onto the scrapbook paper with a pencil (A). Cut letters out of paper with a craft knife.

4 Apply cut-out letter papers to prepared wood letters using Mod Podge Matte. Brush a layer of Mod Podge onto the wood letters' fronts as well as onto the wrong side of the paper letters. Position paper letter on wood letter, and smooth in place. Cut or rip Mod Podge Podgeable paper to size and apply to the letters in random places using Mod Podge Matte.

5 Cut papers with inspiring words to fit Mod Podge Podgeable Metal Blanks, and apply papers with Mod Podge Matte. When dry, apply Mod Podge Clear Dimensional Magic to fill the blanks. Allow to dry. Using the Mod Podge Mod Melter, attach paper flowers to tops of the Mod Podge Metal Blanks.

6 Attach a metal blank and paper flower to each of the wooden LOVE letters with Mod Podge Mod Melts.

CONFETTI BOWL

DESIGNER: *Julieta Martinez*

Make this colorful and fun bowl, and have fun enjoying the process!

WHAT YOU'LL NEED MOD PODGE SPARKLE ☐ ROUND REGULAR-SIZE BALLOON ☐ PLASTIC OR GLASS VASE, APPROXIMATELY 5 INCHES (12.7 CM) DIAMETER, TO HOLD DRYING BALLOON ☐ BAG OF CONFETTI, APPROXIMATELY 1.75 QUARTS (1.7 L) ☐ NEWSPAPER ☐ SPONGE BRUSH (MEDIUM SIZE) ☐ NEEDLE ☐ SCISSORS

WHAT YOU'LL DO

1 Inflate the balloon according to the size you want your completed bowl to be.

2 Use newspaper to cover your workspace, and then pour the confetti over it.

Note: Confetti Bowl for non-food use only.

3 Using a sponge brush, apply Mod Podge Sparkle on the top half of the balloon (A).

4 Roll the Mod Podged balloon over the confetti, pressing the confetti to the balloon (B).

CONFETTI BOWL

5 Add another coat of Mod Podge Sparkle and repeat step 4, until the balloon is almost covered in confetti. Rest the confetti-covered balloon upside down over a vase (C). Allow to dry at least 2 hours.

6 Add one or two more coats of Mod Podge Sparkle and confetti, until the balloon is fully covered. Let it dry on the vase for 2 more hours.

7 Pop the balloon with a needle.

8 The raw edge of the confetti bowl can be trimmed using scissors for a clean, straight edge—or leave as is, to allow a more random effect.

C

OH SO STYLISH

Here are some trendy, beyond-the-basics home decor and gift projects for the avid professional crafter; these projects require greater skill and time commitment than earlier ones.

THE BIG BOOK OF MOD PODGE®

ROCK'N' GUITAR ART

DESIGNER: *Andrea Currie*

Upcycle an old guitar into a beautiful work of art, with little more than paper scraps and sparkly findings.

WHAT YOU'LL NEED MOD PODGE BASIC TOOL KIT (PAGE 18) ▪ MOD PODGE FURNITURE GLOSS ▪ MOD PODGE MOD MELT, SEA GLASS CLEAR ▪ MOD PODGE MOD MOLD, ALPHABET ▪ MOD PODGE ROCKS! PEEL & STICK STENCIL, STARLITE ▪ MOD PODGE SPOUNCER SET ▪ OLD GUITAR ▪ AT LEAST 4 DIFFERENT THIN PAPERS IN VARIOUS PATTERNS (SPECIALTY GIFTWRAP WORKS GREAT FOR THIS) ▪ ACRYLIC MULTI-SURFACE PRIMER (IF YOUR PAPER IS TRANSPARENT AND GUITAR IS DARK) ▪ FINE OPAQUE GLITTER (IN COORDINATING COLORS) ▪ 2 YARDS (1.8 M) FAKE RHINESTONE RIBBON (8 ROWS OF RHINESTONES WORKS THE BEST) ▪ VARIOUS RHINESTONES AND EMBELLISHMENTS OF CHOICE ▪ 2 YARDS (1.8 M) OF STRING OR YARN ▪ MOD PODGE MOD MELTER

WHAT YOU'LL DO

1 Remove the hardware and strings from the guitar.

2 Mod Podge a piece of test paper to the back of the guitar with Mod Podge Furniture Gloss. If it becomes too transparent, paint white multi-surface primer all over the guitar to cover the dark color, and allow it to dry.

3 Cut decorative paper into 1-inch-wide (2.5 cm) strips. With thin layers of Mod Podge Furniture Gloss, add strips to guitar in alternating patterns and lengths. Overlap the edges by ½ inch (1.3 cm). Smooth paper out with fingers.

4 Fold paper over edges of guitar with a dab of Mod Podge Furniture Gloss, and smooth out.

5 Appy a top coat of Mod Podge Furniture Gloss to entire guitar surface.

6 After Mod Podge is fully dry, cover exposed areas (top of neck, sides of guitar) with Mod Podge Furniture Gloss and quickly sprinkle with glitter (A). Repeat on areas that are still exposed. Allow to dry completely.

7 Use Mod Podge Rocks! Peel & Stick Stencil to add glittery shapes to body of guitar, by stenciling on Mod Podge Furniture Gloss, removing the stencil while Mod Podge is still wet, and sprinkling on glitter.

8 Once the glitter and Mod Podge layer is fully dry, add a protective layer of Mod Podge Furniture Gloss over the entire guitar. Be extra gentle when adding Mod Podge over the glittered areas. Switch brushes if glitter builds up on current brush.

9 Measure circumference of guitar with string, and cut rhinestone ribbon to length. Depending on the size and rows of rhinestone ribbon desired, ribbon may be cut down to three or two rows wide. Use hot glue to adhere rhinestone ribbon to edges of guitar (B).

10 Cut a single row out of remaining rhinestone ribbon and adhere to guitar frets. Three rows of rhinestone ribbon should also work for the string knobs at the top.

11 Add embellishments where desired. Use Mod Podge Alphabet Mod Mold and Mod Podge Mod Melt to create fun phrases or names. Top off with coordinating rhinestones using either hot glue or white craft glue.

MOSAIC TILE JEWELRY BOX

DESIGNER: *Chris Williams*

Small squares of paper can quickly resemble mosaic tile when Mod Podged to a box and then embellished with Mod Podge Dimensional Magic.

WHAT YOU'LL NEED MOD PODGE BASIC TOOL KIT (PAGE 18) ☐ MOD PODGE MATTE ☐ MOD PODGE DIMENSIONAL MAGIC, CLEAR ☐ FOLKART MULTI-SURFACE PAINT: STEEL GRAY AND LICORICE ☐ WOOD JEWELRY BOX ☐ ASSORTED COORDINATING SCRAPBOOK PAPERS (HOT PINK PAPER, AND HOT PINK-AND-BLACK PATTERNED PAPERS IN MODEL) ☐ GRIDDED CUTTING MAT ☐ METAL STRAIGHT EDGE RULER ☐ FINE-GRIT SANDPAPER ☐ VERY SMALL SCREWDRIVER TO REMOVE JEWELRY BOX HARDWARE

WHAT YOU'LL DO

1 Start your project by removing the hardware (metal feet, handle, hinges, and clasp) using a very small screwdriver. This step will make it easier for you to paint and Mod Podge, rather than working around the metal hardware. So none of the pieces are lost, place all hardware, including tiny screws, in a bowl for safekeeping.

2 Each side of the box will be covered by one solid piece of scrapbook paper. To create a pattern, lay one side of the box on the wrong side of the scrapbook paper. Using a pencil trace around the box side. Remove the box and cut the pattern shape. Repeat for the remaining three sides.

3 To create ½-inch-square (1.3 cm) paper mosaic tiles, lay the desired scrapbook paper flat on a cutting mat. Position the metal ruler ½ inch (1.3 cm) from the paper's edge and cut along the metal edge, using a craft knife. Continue cutting ½-inch (1.3 cm) strips. Then cut each strip into ½-inch-square (1.3 cm) paper tiles. Create paper tiles from two different papers (pink and pink-and-black paper in model). Set aside.

4 All areas that will be decorated with a mosaic paper tiles should be basecoated with FolkArt Multi-Surface Paint in Steel Gray, which will resemble grout. Accent areas, such as top edge of lid, should be basecoated with FolkArt Multi-Surface Paint in Licorice. Allow paint to dry; sand paint smooth, using fine-grit sandpaper, and reapply base colors. Let dry.

5 Now that your box is basecoated and your paper shapes have been cut, begin decoupaging the paper to the box itself. Start with the box itself, positioning the paper and then Mod Podging it in place using basic Mod Podge techniques and Mod Podge Matte.

6 Create a mosaic tile pattern on the box lid by moving the paper tiles around until you have a pattern that suits you. With Mod Podge Matte, decoupage each paper tile down in place where desired, working, one paper tile at a time (A). Remember to allow some of the basecoated color between the tiles to show through, to represent the grout. Apply a coat of Mod Podge Matte over the entire box and lid, after papers have been applied. Allow to dry.

7 Creating the dimensional look of tile is so much fun using Mod Podge Clear Dimensional Magic. Simply outline each square using the writer tip of the bottle by touching the paper tile and lightly squeeze and direct the flow (B). Mod Podge Dimensional Magic will stay put and will not spill over beyond the square paper tile. Keep your project flat and level while drying. When completed, each paper tile will have the look and feel of glazed ceramic tiles!

8 Before replacing the metal hardware, brush a touch of FolkArt Multi-Surface Paint in Licorice over each piece to tone down the shiny brass. Allow to dry before replacing them. Replace the metal hardware and enjoy!

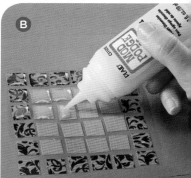

WHIMSICAL BIRD MOBILE

DESIGNER: **DEBBIE SAENZ**

WHIMSICAL BIRD MOBILE

This whimsical mobile is sure to capture your child's imagination with its many colors and textures of birds and hearts, dancing around under a canopy of colorful ribbons and flowers.

WHAT YOU'LL NEED MOD PODGE GLOSS ▪ POSTER BOARD ▪ WOOD FOR MAKING BIRDS ¼-INCH (6 MM) THICK (OR 6 WOODEN BIRD CUTOUTS) ▪ SCROLL SAW (IF CUTTING WOOD) ▪ 5 WOOD HEARTS (TO DANGLE FROM BIRDS) ▪ 6 DECORATIVE SCRAPBOOK PAPERS (DIFFERENT COLORS) ▪ 6 ACRYLIC PAINT COLORS TO MATCH PAPERS) ▪ 6 PIECES OF FELT (TO COORDINATE WITH PAPERS) ▪ 60 COLORFUL RHINESTONES ▪ MOD PODGE WONDER GLUE ▪ 12 SMALL SCREW EYES ▪ 24 COLORFUL BEADS ▪ 24 EYE PINS ▪ 18 LARGE JUMP RINGS ▪ WIRE HANGING GARDEN PLANTER ▪ MONOFILAMENT (TO ATTACH THINGS) ▪ VARIETY OF COLORFUL RIBBONS ▪ 1-INCH-WIDE (2.5 CM) GREEN RIBBON OR LACE ▪ 12 ARTIFICIAL FLOWERS ▪ FINE-GRIT SANDPAPER ▪ DISTRESSING INK AND BLENDING TOOL ▪ TEMPLATES FOR BIRD AND HEART (PAGE 233) ▪ PENCIL ▪ ¾ INCH (19 MM) FLAT BRUSH ▪

WHAT YOU'LL DO

1 Using bird pattern provided in the Templates section, draw six birds on wood and cut out with scroll saw (or use precut wooden birds).

2 Paint the edges of each bird and heart with a different color.

3 Working one side of the wood cutouts at a time, adhere papers to each bird and heart using Mod Podge Gloss, and allow to dry. Sand off all extra paper that extends beyond the edges with sandpaper (A; see page 106). Repeat for other side of each wood cutout. Distress the edges of both sides with distressing ink and distressing blending tool. Seal both sides with a coat of Mod Podge Gloss, and allow to dry.

4 Cut two wings for each bird from felt and attach to each side of birds with Mod Podge Wonder Glue. Next attach rhinestones to each side of birds and hearts with Mod Podge Wonder Glue.

5 For hanging birds, insert screw eyes at top of back and bottom of breast of each bird. Make holes in top center of each heart.

6 Thread beads on eye pin, creating a bead charm or link. Make six links of 3 beads each, using eye pins. Attach a 3-bead link to top of each bird with a jump ring. Make six 1-bead links and attach to bottom of each bird. Attach hearts with jump rings below one-bead links.

7 Reattach the chain from the top of the wire basket to the basket's bottom to create a hanger for the basket.

8 Tie a 24-inch (61 cm) piece of monofilament to the top of each bird and charm dangle. Tie one bird to hang from the center of the basket. Tie the remaining five birds evenly spaced around outside edge of basket.

9 Cut ribbons approximately 5 inches (12.7 cm) in length and tie onto the edges of basket. Randomly tie 12 pieces of green 1-inch-wide (2.5 cm) ribbon or lace around top and sides of basket. Glue flowers in the centers of the ribbons.

WHIMSICAL BIRD MOBILE

HELPFUL SUGGESTIONS/ALTERNATIVE IDEAS

- Purchase precut wooden birds instead of cutting them out. Use flowers or any other shape instead of birds. (If you are using very thin wood, drill holes and use jump rings instead of screw eyes.)

- Use wood bird as a template to trace on wrong side of paper, then cut out.

- Adhere papers to one side of bird and heart and sand off edges before adhering paper to the opposite side.

- Hang the basket after reattaching the chain for easier access while attaching and adjusting birds.

- Use a birdcage to hang the birds on instead of a garden basket.

A

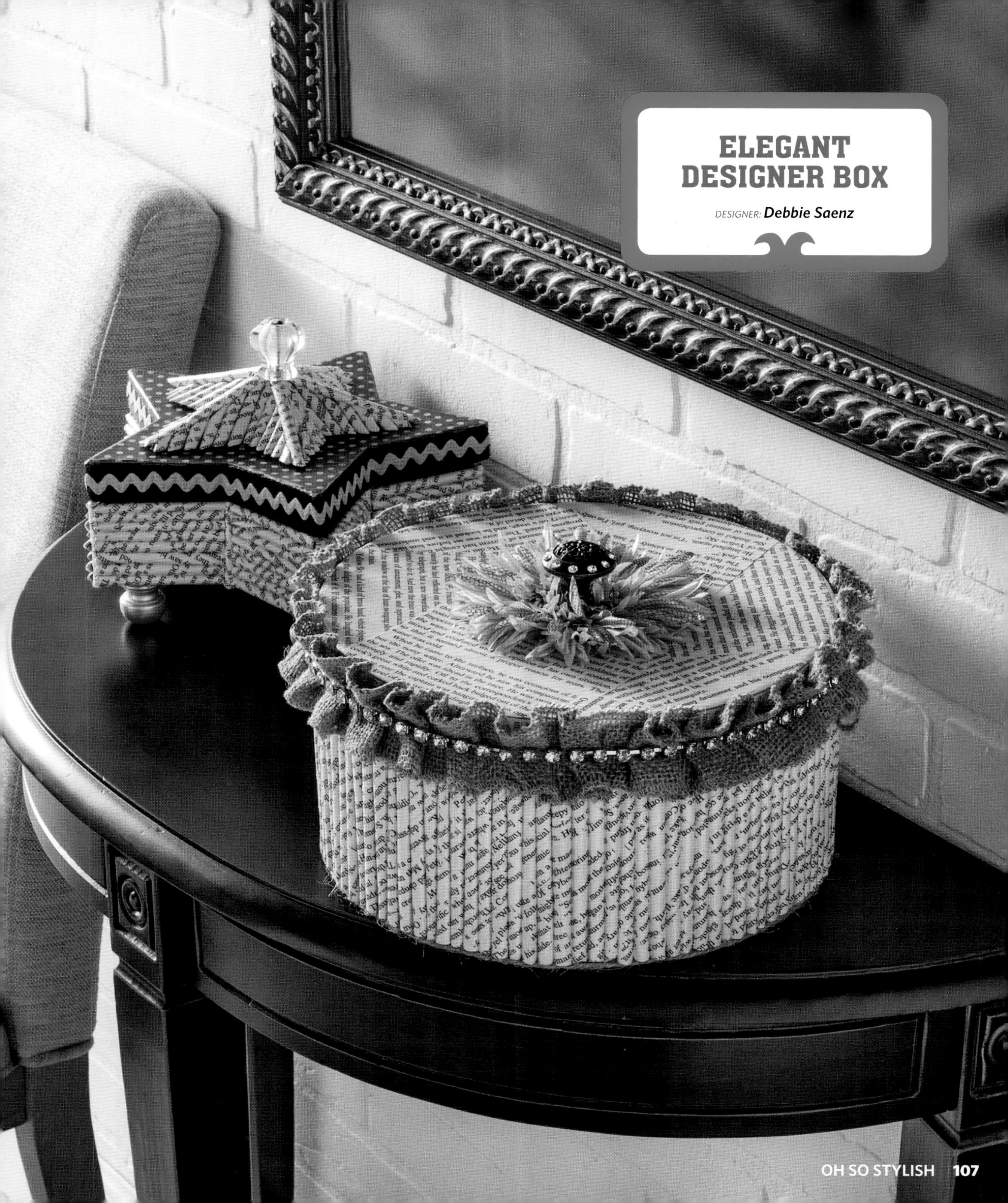

ELEGANT DESIGNER BOX

DESIGNER: ***Debbie Saenz***

ELEGANT DESIGNER BOX

Burlap and rhinestones complement the rolled book pages, making this box a statement piece of elegance. Change the trim, flower, and knob for a totally different look!

WHAT YOU'LL NEED MOD PODGE BASIC TOOL KIT (PAGE 18) ☐ MOD PODGE GLOSS ☐ ROUND PAPIER-MÂCHÉ BOX ☐ OLD BOOK PAGES ☐ NARROW DOWEL ROD OR (WOODEN KABOB SKEWER) ☐ DISTRESSING INK ☐ JUTE TWINE ☐ BURLAP RUFFLE TRIM (WITH RHINESTONES) ☐ CREAM-COLORED SILK FLOWER ☐ DECORATIVE KNOB (WITH RHINESTONES) ☐ MOD PODGE MOD MELTER ☐ MOD PODGE MOD MELTS, CLEAR

WHAT YOU'LL DO

1 Cut page out of book and trim to remove all margins up to print. Use a small dowel to roll up paper. Place the dowel just over one corner of the page and tightly roll paper around dowel (A). Use Mod Podge Gloss to adhere outer edge of paper, keeping the paper rolled up. Once secure, allow to dry, then remove the dowel. Continue making paper rolls until you have enough to cover base of box.

2 With lid on the box, draw a line around the outside of the box base just under the lid. Measure and cut paper rolls to fit from the drawn line to the bottom of box. Adhere rolled papers to box with Mod Podge Mod Melt. Seal with a generous coat of Mod Podge Gloss.

3 Use Mod Podge Gloss to adhere unrolled book pages flat to top and side edge of lid, overlapping pages. Sand off extra paper that extends beyond the lid. Distress edges with distressing ink. Seal top of lid only with a coat of Mod Podge Gloss; allow to dry.

4 Use Mod Podge Mod Melt to adhere ruffle around side of box lid.

5 Create a hole in box lid center using craft knife. Remove and discard center part of flower; insert knob into flower and attach to box lid.

6 Use Mod Podge Mod Melt to glue three strands of jute twine to top edge and bottom edge of paper rolls for a finished look.

BONUS PROJECT

SPECTACULAR STAR BOX

The pages on this box jump right out at you! A dimensional star-shaped ornament is the base on which I built a 3D star embellishment to turn this ordinary star box into something spectacular!

WHAT YOU'LL NEED MOD PODGE BASIC TOOL KIT (PAGE 18) ▪ MOD PODGE MATTE ▪ FOLKART ACRYLIC PAINT: LICORICE AND METALLIC AQUAMARINE ▪ PAPIER-MÂCHÉ STAR BOX ▪ FOUR 1¹⁄₁₆-INCH (2.7 CM) FINIAL DOWEL CAPS (FOR FEET) ▪ SHEET OF BLACK POLKA DOT PAPER 12 x 12 INCHES (30.5 x 30.5 CM) ▪ DISTRESSING INK ▪ OLD BOOK PAGES ▪ SCISSORS ▪ SMALL DOWEL ROD ▪ MOD PODGE MOD MELTER ▪ MOD PODGE MOD MELTS, CLEAR ▪ PAPIER-MÂCHÉ STAR ORNAMENT FOR LID ▪ MOD PODGE WONDER GLUE ▪ RICKRACK GREEN ▪ GREEN GLASS DRAWER KNOB ▪ PENCIL ▪ SANDPAPER

WHAT YOU'LL DO

1 With lid on the box, draw a line around the outside of the box base just under the lid. Paint the outside of the box above the line, the inside of the box, the inside of the lid, the outside edge of the box lid, and the bottom of the box with FolkArt Acrylic Paint in Licorice. Paint the dowel caps FolkArt Acrylic Paint in Metallic Aquamarine.

2 Use lid to trace a star on back of polka dot paper. Cut out and adhere paper to lid with Mod Podge Matte. Sand off extra paper that extends beyond edges. Distress the edges with distressing ink. Seal with a coat of Mod Podge Matte, allow to dry.

3 Cut pages out of book and trim all margins off, up to print area. Use a narrow dowel to roll up paper. Place the dowel just over one corner and tightly roll paper around dowel. Use Mod Podge Matte to adhere end of paper, keeping the paper in a roll. Slide paper off dowel, and continue making paper rolls until you have more than enough to cover the surfaces of the star box sides.

4 Measure and cut 10 paper rolls to fit vertically, one each on each inner and outer angle of the star for the base of box, extending up to just under painted line. Adhere the 10 rolls

to box with Mod Podge Mod Melter and Mod Podge Mod Melts. Then measure and cut paper rolls to fit horizontally between each pair of vertical paper rolls on base of box. Cut one end of each roll on a 45-degree angle and place that end on the outer edge (point) of star. Adhere horizontal rolls with hot Mod Podge Mod Melt. Seal all paper rolls onto box base with a generous coat of Mod Podge Matte.

5 Cut papier-mâché star ornament in half to allow star to lie flat. Use hot Mod Podge Mod Melt to adhere paper rolls on inner and outer angles of star edge (see photo for reference). Cut ends at an angle. Fill in remaining star sections with paper rolls, and cut ends at an angle. Seal entire star with a generous coat of Mod Podge Matte.

6 Adhere rickrack to edge of box lid with Mod Podge Matte. Seal with Mod Podge Matte. For feet, glue a dowel cap to bottom of box on each star point with hot Mod Podge Mod Melt.

7 Make hole in center of star ornament and insert glass knob. Secure with screw or glue. Use Mod Podge Wonder Glue to attach star to center of lid top. Let everything dry before using box.

HOME IS WHERE THE HEART IS

DESIGNER: **Kirsten Jones**

HOME is where the ♥ is...

Anyone can paint with some cute paper and a canvas!

WHAT YOU'LL NEED MOD PODGE BASIC TOOL KIT (PAGE 18) ◼ MOD PODGE SATIN ◼ FOLKART ACRYLIC PAINT: WICKER WHITE, LICORICE, LIGHT BLUE, PATINA, LIME GREEN, YELLOW LEMON, AND NUTMEG ◼ 11 x 14 INCH (28 x 36 CM) STRETCHED CANVAS ◼ NO. 1 LINER BRUSH ◼ NO. 10 FLAT BRUSH ◼ NO. 4 FLAT BRUSH ◼ WHITE CHALK ◼ ASSORTED SCRAPBOOK PAPERS (FOR HOUSE, ROOF, TREE, AND HEART) ◼ TEMPLATES (PAGE 230)

WHAT YOU'LL DO

1 Basecoat canvas with FolkArt Acrylic Paint in Licorice; let dry.

2 Lightly sketch design onto painted canvas using white chalk if desired to determine the size of all elements that are paper (house, tree, roof, and heart) or use patterns provided in the template section of the book.

3 Cut the scrapbook paper and lay out design onto canvas where desired. With Mod Podge Satin, adhere the papers to the canvas, using a flat brush. Let dry.

4 Next, using the FolkArt Acrylic Paints, paint around the papers, creating the background. The sky is painted Wicker White, Light Blue, and Patina; use very loose brushstrokes to get the variation in the sky color (A). Paint grass areas Lime Green and Wicker White, overlapping strokes. The tree trunk is painted Nutmeg, and the door is Yellow Lemon. Let all paint dry.

5 With the small flat brush, add the checked pattern onto the edge of the canvas, using FolkArt Acrylic Paint in Licorice and Wicker White. Let dry.

6 Using the liner brush, randomly outline all paper pieces and add accents where desired (B). Personalize with words "HOME is where the ♥ is." Let dry.

MOD PODGE FABRIC SUITCASE

DESIGNER: **Sherrie Ragsdale**

Dress up the airport with this funky patterned suitcase.

WHAT YOU'LL NEED MOD PODGE BASIC TOOL KIT (PAGE 18) ◼ MOD PODGE FABRIC ◼ KRAFT PAPER FOR PATTERN ◼ BRIGHTLY COLORED SUITCASE ◼ BRIGHTLY COLORED FABRIC (LARGE ENOUGH TO COVER SUITCASE)

WHAT YOU'LL DO

1 Cover the wrong side of the fabric with the Mod Podge Fabric (A). Allow to dry.

2 Determine areas of suitcase to be covered with fabric. Make paper patterns for those areas of the suitcase, before cutting fabric. Use the patterns to cut the prepared fabric to fit within these areas.

3 Adhere cut fabric sections to suitcase with Mod Podge Fabric. Allow to dry. Apply a finishing protective top coat of Mod Podge Fabric. Allow to dry.

BLUE BIRD

GOLDFISH

FLAMINGO

PINK

Create colorful works of art with an array of paint-chip swatches found at the local paint store.

WHAT YOU'LL NEED MOD PODGE BASIC TOOL KIT (PAGE 18) ■ MOD PODGE MATTE ■ FOLKART ACRYLIC PAINT: BABY PINK, YELLOW LEMON, LIGHT BLUE, LICORICE, COFFEE BEAN, AND WICKER WHITE ■ 24 x 48 INCH (61 x 122 CM) BIRCH PLYWOOD ■ TRANSFER OR TRACING PAPER ■ POSTER BOARD, ONE LARGE SHEET ■ PAINT SAMPLE SWATCHES: SHADES OF ORANGE, YELLOW, BLUE, PINK, MAGENTA ■ 1½-INCH (1.3 CM) ALPHABET PAPER STENCILS ■ STENCIL BRUSH ■ 3 WIGGLE EYES (DESIRED SIZE), ONE FOR EACH ANIMAL ■ MOD PODGE MOD MELTER ■ MOD PODGE MOD MELT, SEA GLASS CLEAR ■ TEMPLATES FOR BLUEBIRD, FLAMINGO, AND GOLDFISH (PAGES 233, 234)

WHAT YOU'LL DO

1 For plaques, cut one rectangle out of the plywood 15 x 10¼ inches (38.1 x 26 cm); basecoat using FolkArt Acrylic Paint in Baby Pink. Cut another plaque 12 x 8 inches (30.5 x 20.3 cm); basecoat using FolkArt Acrylic Paint in Yellow Lemon. Cut a third plaque 12 x 18 inches (30.5 x 45.7 cm); basecoat it using FolkArt Acrylic Paint in Light Blue. Allow them to dry and then sand to distress all three plaques.

2 Using the patterns provided in the Template section of book, trace the animal patterns onto tracing paper and cut them out. Trace around the pattern pieces onto poster board (A), leaving a few inches of room around each tracing, but do not cut these pieces out of the poster board yet.

3 For the goldfish, cut small pieces of paper, about ½ inch (1.3 cm) square (B), from various shades of yellow and orange paint chips (see photo for color guide to parts of fish). Just follow the colors in the order that they are on the paint chips themselves, using the photo for reference. Mod Podge the cut paint-chip squares onto the poster board pattern piece, beginning at the bottom of each pattern piece. Layer the paint-chip squares, starting with darker shades and working toward the lighter while moving upward on the pattern. Be sure to place each outer-edge

PAINT-CHIP WALL ART

square directly on top of the pattern outline (C). Once the layers have been applied and are dry, place the pattern piece tracing on top of the Mod Podged poster board and trace around pattern (D). Cut out the pattern piece through the layers of paper.

4 For bluebird and flamingo, repeat procedure, using the same techniques as for goldfish, working with pink and magenta paint chips for the flamingo and blue chips for the bluebird.

5 Place the bluebird on the yellow plaque, the flamingo on the blue plaque, and the goldfish on the pink plaque. Adjust spacing for the stenciled words and animal parts (beaks and legs), and bubbles. Lightly mark position of animal in pencil, and remove the pattern pieces from each board to stencil word, using FolkArt Acrylic Paint, in Licorice. Using FolkArt Acrylic Paints, paint the bluebird's beak Licorice and the feet Coffee Bean. Use Coffee Bean for the flamingo's feet and Wicker White for the beak, with Licorice at the tip. Color the goldfish's bubbles Light Blue. Allow to dry.

6 Once paint is dry, adhere the paint-chip animals to each plaque using the Mod Podge Mod Melter and Mod Podge Mod Melt. Glue wiggle eye to each animal.

old self again. The
absolutely furious
mbers very little of
ll out, turning and
or me to erase the
ind. At least she's
up to see her, but
ning. It seems the
he ran off without
erhaps it wasn't a
of was a caterpil-
ey don't know our
s for bed pan and I
t. Meanwhile she's
aff and has earned
s for bed pan and I

DECORATOR PATTERNED PAPER BOX SET

These are great places to store jewelry and other small trinkets.

WHAT YOU'LL NEED ☐ MOD PODGE BASIC TOOL KIT (PAGE 18) ☐ MOD PODGE PAPER MATTE ☐ FOLKART ACRYLIC PAINT, DEEP OCEAN BLUE ☐ 3 PAPIER-MÂCHÉ BOXES: VARIOUS SIZES AND SHAPES ☐ ASSORTED BLUE SCRAPBOOK PAPERS (LINES, SQUARES, AND POLKA DOTS). ☐ ½-INCH (13 MM) FLAT PAINTBRUSH ☐ TRACING PAPER ☐ SPOOL OF WHITE COTTON TWINE ☐ ½-INCH (13 MM) DAUBER ☐ 3 SILVER BUTTERFLIES ☐ DIAMOND PATTERN AND CHEVRON PATTERN TEMPLATES (PAGE 229) ☐ POSTER BOARD ☐ MOD PODGE MOD MELTER ☐ MOD PODGE MOD MELT, CLEAR

NOTE: *Use scrapbook papers that repeat linear patterns. Some can be a polka dot patterns if they are designed in a straight line. Use design lines as a guide to follow when cutting.*

WHAT YOU'LL DO

1 Basecoat outside of all three boxes, including lids, using FolkArt Acrylic Paint in Deep Ocean Blue; allow to dry.

WOVEN BASKET PATTERN

2 Cut ½-inch-wide (1.3 cm) strips following the linear design lines, if possible. Or use a ruler and mark cutting lines. Cut each strip about 2 inches (5 cm) longer than the width of the box lid. On a piece of poster board, line up one set of strips side by side horizontally and glue the ends at left to the poster board. This will hold the strips down while you weave. Begin weaving paper strips vertically into the horizontal strips, alternating where you start each row above or below the horizontal strips (A). After the paper is woven, brush a light coat of Mod Podge Paper Matte over top to hold the weave in place. Once dry, place the box lid onto the woven papers, and then trace around the lid with a pencil. Cut out the woven paper along the pencil line, and Mod Podge the woven paper to the box top using basic Mod Podge techniques. Allow to dry. Wrap white cotton twine a couple times around the box base, brushing Mod Podge on the box as the twine is wrapped. Allow to dry. Apply FolkArt Acrylic Paint in Deep Ocean Blue in dots over the twine, using a ½-inch (13 mm) dauber. Hot-glue butterfly embellishment on box lid.

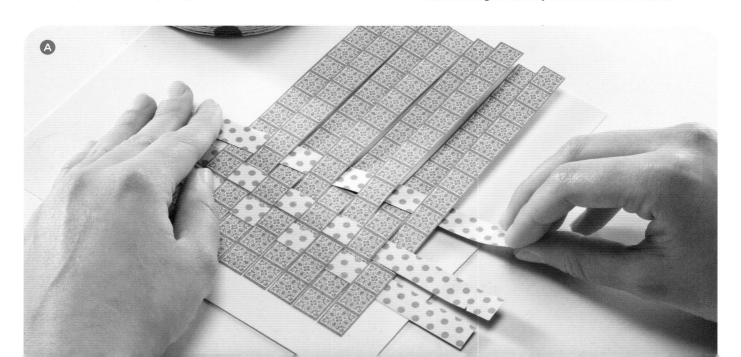

DIAMOND PATTERN BOX

1 Using the diamond pattern found in the Template section and a pencil, trace diamond shape onto tracing paper and cut a pattern. Trace and then cut from scrapbook paper as many diamonds as are needed to fill box lid. Individually Mod Podge paper diamonds onto box lid. Allow to dry. Trim excess paper extending from top of lid. Place lid on box; then measure the portion of the box side that is showing below the lid overhang. Cut coordinating paper this width and long enough to wrap around the box bottom. Mod Podge paper to box bottom. Glue a single wrap of twine at the paper's top edge on the box (but not covered by lid). Using Mod Podge Mod Melt, glue butterfly embellishment to center of the box. Cut small pieces of white cotton twine, and create individual knots from twine; fray twine ends. Using Mod Podge Mod Melt, attach knots to points where diamonds touch on lid.

CHEVRON PATTERN BOX

1 Using the chevron pattern found in the Template section and a pencil, trace chevron shape onto tracing paper and cut out. Trace onto scrapbook paper, and then cut out as many chevrons as needed to fill box lid (B). Individually Mod Podge paper chevrons onto the box lid. Allow to dry. Trim excess paper extending from top of lid. Cut a strip of paper long enough to wrap around the box base and as tall as half the box base's height. Apply paper strip to box base with Mod Podge. Allow to dry. Wrap the middle of the box with a few rounds of white cotton twine, covering the top edge of paper, Mod Podging it in place as you wrap. Glue on butterfly embellishment near twine (see photo on page 117).

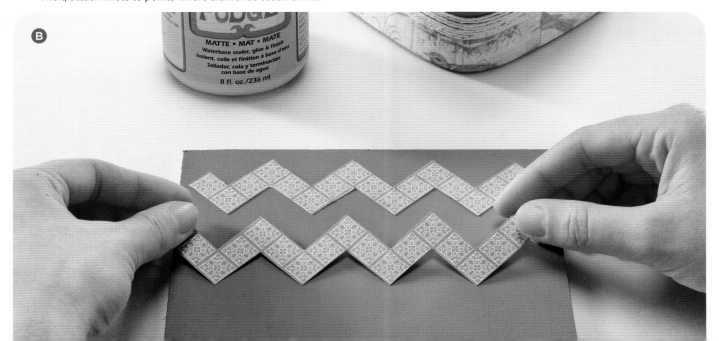

PICTURE PERFECT PILLOWS

DESIGNER: **Walter Silva**

PICTURE PERFECT PILLOWS

I've been collecting vintage toys for decades. I'm always excited to share my collection on social media, and I can decorate my home with my photos of my favorite finds.

WHAT YOU'LL NEED MOD PODGE PHOTO TRANSFER MEDIUM ▪ PHOTO AND LASER PHOTOCOPY OF PHOTO (SEE DETAILS IN STEP 2) ▪ 1-INCH (2.5 CM) FOAM PAINTBRUSH ▪ FOAM CORE BOARD ▪ 16 x 16-INCH (40.6 x 40.6 CM) DECORATIVE PILLOW (WITH REMOVABLE PILLOW FORM), OR WHATEVER SIZE PILLOW YOU WANT ▪ WAXED PAPER ▪ SPONGE ▪ SCISSORS ▪ CRAFT KNIFE ▪ TAPE

WHAT YOU'LL DO

1 Remove pillow form and wash pillow cover; allow to dry. Then iron to remove wrinkles.

2 Select your favorite digital image. Using photo-editing software, size the image to fit your project surface, and then laser-print the image. If you don't have photo-editing software, you can have an image altered at a copy center. Remember to ask for a mirror image or reversed copy, especially if the photo features words.

3 Cut a piece of foam core board slightly bigger than the photocopy; cover one side with waxed paper. Insert it into the pillow cover, with the waxed paper facing the front of the pillow. This will protect the back of the pillow, should Mod Podge Photo Transfer Medium seep through.

4 Cut the laser copy to the desired size; apply a smooth, medium-to-thick coat of Mod Podge Photo Transfer Medium directly onto the right side of the image, using a foam brush. Cover the entire image so that the image cannot be seen.

5 Being careful not to touch the image, flip it over and place it directly onto the front of the pillow. Press the laser copy paper onto the pillow from the center of the design outward to make sure the entire piece is adhered without air pockets. Allow to dry, waiting 24 hours before the next step.

6 Using a moistened sponge, wring out excess water, but not all water. Saturate the back of the paper transfer; like magic you will start to see the image. Wait two minutes.

7 Then take the moistened sponge and start to lightly rub in a circular motion. Layers of the paper will start to peel away. Note: You may also use your wet fingers too. Once it seems all paper has been removed, allow the pillow to dry. When dry, if any paper remains, white paper fibers will be seen on the image. Repeat process of wetting and lightly rubbing to remove remaining paper fibers. Allow to dry. Repeat process, if necessary.

8 Remove the waxed-paper–covered foam core board; slide the pillowform into the pillow cover. Ready for use!

DIY FASHION

Here are wearables, accessories, jewelry, and more,
created or embellished with Mod Podge.

THE BIG BOOK OF MOD PODGE®

FAUX CROCODILE CIGAR BOX PURSE

DESIGNER: *Candie Cooper*

FAUX CROCODILE CIGAR BOX PURSE

Creating a purse from an unexpected item is tons of fun and so fashionable!

WHAT YOU'LL NEED MOD PODGE BASIC TOOL KIT (PAGE 18) ■ MOD PODGE ANTIQUE MATTE ■ MOD PODGE MATTE ■ FOLKART ACRYLIC PAINTS: REAL BROWN AND ROSE SHIMMER ■ WOODEN CIGAR BOX ■ TWO 12 x 12-INCH (30.5 x 30.5 CM) CROCODILE-EMBOSSED SCRAPBOOK PAPERS, OR WHATEVER SIZE WILL FIT THE TOP AND BOTTOM SURFACES OF THE BOX ■ 36-INCH (91 CM) LINEN RIBBON ■ COLOR COPIES OF VINTAGE IMAGES: LARGE ONES FOR INSIDE PURSE AND SMALL FLORAL ONES FOR BUTTONS ■ 3 LARGE BUTTONS, TO DECORATE LID ■ FLAT-BACK CRYSTALSD ■ MOD PODGE MOD MELTER ■ MOD PODGE MOD MELTS, SEA GLASS CLEAR

WHAT YOU'LL DO

1 Basecoat the cigar purse using FolkArt Acrylic Paint in Real Brown on the outside and Metallic Rose Shimmer on the inside. Allow to dry.

2 Using a pencil, trace the box shape onto the crocodile scrapbook paper and cut out—one each for the top and bottom.

3 Apply a coat of Mod Podge Matte onto outer surface of lid of the box, and press the crocodile paper into place (A). Repeat for the bottom of the box. Seal with a layer of Mod Podge Matte.

4 Cut out the vintage images. Use Mod Podge Antique Matte to adhere them to the inside of the box, and paint over images with Mod Podge Antique Matte (B). Let dry.

5 Apply dots of Mod Podge Antique Matte around the images and place flat-back crystals on top of dots. Keep them flat and allow to dry.

6 Measure and cut two pieces of ribbon, to be glued flat on the outside center of the box, one on the lid and one around the box base. Take care to leave ½ inch (1.3 cm) extra ribbon on each piece for turning the edges under.

7 Turn the ribbon under ¼ inch (6 mm) and secure end of ribbon with Mod Podge Mod Melter and Mod Podge Mod Melt. Repeat for the opposite end of ribbon.

8 Glue the ribbons to the center of the box on the lid and around the bottom of the box.

9 Cut the vintage flower images so they fit the center of three large buttons. Mod Podge them to the center each button. Once the images are adhered and dry, add a coat of Mod Podge Antique Matte to seal and protect them (C).

10 Using the Mod Podge Mod Melter and Mod Podge Mold Melt, glue the buttons to the center of the ribbon.

FAUX OILCLOTH FLOWER BROOCH

Fashionable pins can be found everywhere, but it is so much more fun to create your own. Wear your fashionable flower pin on a scarf, purse, jacket, or sweater. Create to share with friends.

WHAT YOU'LL NEED MOD PODGE FABRIC ◻ MOD PODGE MOD MELT STICKS, MILK GLASS WHITE ◻ MOD PODGE MOD MOLD, FLOWER ◻ DIE CUTTER WITH FLOWER DIE, OR SCISSORS ◻ FABRIC IN DESIRED PRINTS, 1 FAT QUARTER (18 x 22 INCHES, OR 45.7 x 56 CM) OF EACH ◻ MOD PODGE MOD MELTER ◻ MOD PODGE MOD MELTS, SEA GLASS CLEAR ◻ APPLE BARREL ACRYLIC PAINT, COLORS TO MATCH FABRIC ◻ FLAT-BACK EMBELLISHMENT ◻ CRAFT FELT TO FIT BACK OF BROOCH ◻ JEWELRY PIN BACK ◻ ¾-INCH (19 MM) FLAT BRUSH ◻ TEMPLATE (PAGE 231)

WHAT YOU'LL DO

1 Cut flower shapes from fabric using a die cutter or scissors. Cut three different sizes so they fit together concentrically. Cut a wedge from each one, about one-sixth of the circle, so when the flower shapes are glued together they will be three-dimensional (A).

2 Paint a coat of Mod Podge Fabric onto each flower piece and lay them on a nonstick surface to dry.

3 Hot-glue the flower pieces together. Set aside.

4 Load the Mod Podge Mod Melter with a Mod Podge Mod Melt and allow to heat up. Fill a Mod Podge Flower Mod Mold with the heated Mod Podge Mod Melt. Allow to cool completely. Make one for each brooch.

5 When cool, release the embellishment from the Mod Podge Mod Mold and paint desired color. Allow to dry.

6 Glue a flat-back embellishment to the center of the painted Mod Podge Mod Melt flower with the Mod Podge Mod Melter. Then glue the Mod Podge Mod Melt flower embellishment to the center of the fabric flower (B).

7 Cut a circle of felt that fits the back of the fabric flower, and glue in place using hot glue.

8 Hot-glue the jewelry pin back to the back of the fabric flower.

A

B

INDUSTRIAL CHIC STRETCHY CHARM BRACELET

DESIGNER: *Carol Cook*

INDUSTRIAL CHIC STRETCHY CHARM BRACELET

Combine feminine and funky in an easy-to-make stretch bracelet using crystal and metal beads and accented with an industrial charm you create yourself!

WHAT YOU'LL NEED   MOD PODGE MOD MELTER   ■   MOD PODGE MOD MELT, METALLIC GOLD   ■   MOD PODGE MOD MOLD, INDUSTRIAL (FOR LOCK MOLD)   ■   FOLKART ACRYLIC PAINT, SILVER STERLING   ■   STRETCHY BEAD CORD   ■   THIRTEEN 10-MM CRYSTAL BEADS (YOU MAY NEED MORE OR FEWER, DEPENDING ON WRIST SIZE)   ■   THIRTEEN 8-MM METAL BEADS (YOU MAY USE MORE OR FEWER, DEPENDING ON WRIST SIZE)   ■   BINDER CLIP OR CLOTHESPIN   ■   OVAL JEWELRY BEZEL, SIZED TO FIT MOD PODGE MOD MOLD EMBELLISHMENT   ■   FLAT BRUSH   ■   MOD PODGE WONDER GLUE   ■   SMALL JUMP RING, TO ATTACH BEZEL TO BRACELET   ■   SCISSORS

WHAT YOU'LL DO

1 Measure stretchy cord to fit wrist and add 4–6 inches (10–15 cm) so you will be able to tie the ends easily. Clamp one end to prevent beads from sliding off. A binder clip or clothespin works great.

2 String beads onto stretch cord, alternating as desired (A).

3 Join both ends of the bracelet and tie with a knot. Add a dab of Mod Podge Wonder Glue to knot. Tie another knot. Add another dab of glue to seal the knot. Allow Mod Podge Wonder Glue to dry.

4 Make the Mod Podge Mod Mold lock embellishment using the Mod Podge Mod Melter, a Mod Podge Metallic Gold Mod Melt, and the Mod Podge Industrial Mod Mold. When set, drybrush lock with FolkArt Acrylic Paint in Silver Sterling.

5 Using Mod Podge Wonder Glue, glue lock embellishment into oval jewelry bezel to make a charm.

6 Attach charm to bracelet with a jump ring.

PARTY PURSE

DESIGNERS: *Cathie Filian and Steve Piacenza*

PARTY PURSE

Jazz up a plain purse by using Mod Podge Fabric to attach lace appliqués.

WHAT YOU'LL NEED   MOD PODGE FABRIC ◻ KRAFT PAPER OR WAXED PAPER, FOR WORK SURFACE ◻

LACE APPLIQUÉS ◻ STRAIGHT PINS OR QUILTER'S PINS ◻ FOAM PAINTBRUSH ◻ CLUTCH PURSE

WHAT YOU'LL DO

1 Plan the placement of your appliqués on the purse. Mark positioning with a few straight pins or quilter's pins, if necessary. Working one appliqué at a time, place the appliqué right-side down on the covered work surface. Apply Mod Podge Fabric to the backs of the appliqués.

2 Place the appliqués on the purse, one at a time. Smooth with your fingers to remove air bubbles. Press along the edges to create a proper seal (A). Repeat until all appliqués are Mod Podged to the purse where desired.

3 Allow to dry for 4 hours.

MINT-TIN MONEY-HOLDER BELT BUCKLE

The desire to not be burdened by carrying everything in a purse inspired me to turn a simple tin into a decorative, fashionable belt buckle to hold things of importance.

WHAT YOU'LL NEED MOD PODGE BASIC TOOL KIT (PAGE 18) ■ MOD PODGE MATTE ■ MOD PODGE DIMENSIONAL MAGIC, CLEAR ■ FOLKART MULTI-SURFACE PAINT, YOUR CHOICE OF COLOR ■ MINT TIN ■ SCRAPBOOK PAPER ■ PHOTOCOPY SIZED TO FIT THE FACE OR FRONT OF MINT TIN ■ ORNATE METAL PLATE ■ BUCKLE BACK, RING/HOOK ■ DRILL AND NARROW DRILL BIT, TO FIT BOLTS ■ SMALL BOLT SCREWS AND NUTS, TO ATTACH TIN TO BUCKLE BACK ■ MOD PODGE WONDER GLUE

WHAT YOU'LL DO

1 Paint the bottom half of the tin with FolkArt Multi-Surface Paint in color of choice to coordinate with the scrapbook paper of choice. Let dry completely.

2 Trace the shape of the lid onto the back of the scrapbook paper. Cut out shape, leaving approximately ³⁄₁₆ inch (5 mm) extra all around. Brush Mod Podge Matte onto back of paper and place on lid of tin. Smooth out any bubbles with fingers. Cut small slits into edges of paper, to go around curved edges of lid. Smooth until paper is completely adhered.

3 Cut a strip of paper ³⁄₁₆ inch (5 mm) wide. Apply Mod Podge Matte and wrap strip around rim of lid, to cover cut edges of top piece of paper. Let dry at least 20 minutes, and seal lid with several coats of Mod Podge Matte, allowing each coat to dry thoroughly before applying the next.

4 Trim photocopy to fit the opening of the metal plate. Center metal plate on lid of tin, and trace opening with a pencil. Apply Mod Podge Matte to back of photocopy, and place on lid, covering tracing. Seal with Mod Podge Matte.

5 Using Mod Podge Wonder Glue, glue metal plate to lid, covering photocopy. Glue rhinestone gems to metal frame. Fill opening in frame with Mod Podge Dimensional Magic Clear. Keep flat while drying, and allow to dry before applying any additional coats (A).

6 Turn tin over and place buckle back in center of tin back. Mark position of holes with a pencil. Drill holes through tin large enough to match bolt size. Attach buckle back and ring with screws. Place nuts over bolt ends to secure.

A

ARTFUL GLAM JEWELRY

Now here is a project where you can take nothing and create something worthy of any glamour and glitz party! Simple cardstock, some glitzy gems, and Mod Podge Dimensional Magic do the trick.

WHAT YOU'LL NEED MOD PODGE GLOSS ■ MOD PODGE DIMENSIONAL MAGIC, CLEAR ■ CARDSTOCK (PRINTED OR SOLID) ■ SCRAPBOOK PAPER ■ 1 YARD (91.4 CM) OF CUP CHAIN ■ 2 GOLD EARRING POST DISCS (WITH TINY LOOPS) ■ 2 GOLD JUMP RINGS ■ GOLD RING BLANK ■ MOD PODGE WONDER GLUE ■ SCISSORS ■ NEEDLE ■ TEMPLATES OF EARRING SHAPES (PAGE 231)

WHAT YOU'LL DO

EARRINGS

1 Using patterns provided in the Template section of the book, cut out two each of the earring shapes (small square and large teardrop shape), from cardstock. If using patterned cardstock, skip step 2 and move to step 3.

2 If working with solid color cardstock, cut a coordinating patterned scrapbook paper shape for each cardstock piece. Mod Podge the scrapbook pattern paper to the cardstock with Mod Podge Gloss and allow to dry. Apply a topcoat to the scrapbook paper with Mod Podge Gloss; allow to dry.

3 Glue links of cup chain around the outer edge of each of the four earring shapes, using Mod Podge Wonder Glue. Be sure that each section of the cup chain is fully attached to the cardstock. Allow to dry until adhesive is set.

4 Apply Mod Podge Clear Dimensional Magic within the cup chain area, directly on the cutouts of the cardstock or scrapbook paper (A). It is very important to keep each piece fully flat or level while drying. Allow to dry and harden.

5 Once Mod Podge Dimensional Magic is thoroughly dry, use a needle to punch a hole in the top of each teardrop shape. Open a jump ring and feed it through the hole; however, do not close the jump ring—keep it open.

6 Using Mod Podge Wonder Glue, attach the earring post to the back of each square base, setting the earring post in a corner diagonally, and allowing the small loop to overhang at the corner. Allow to dry.

7 Once the post is firmly attached to the back of the earring base, attach the teardrop shape to the earring base. Feed the open jump ring through the small loop at the metal earring base. Close the jump ring.

RING

1 Cut a round shape from cardstock, following the pattern provided in the Template section of the book.

2 Repeat technique steps 2–4 as completed for earrings.

3 Using Mod Podge Wonder Glue, attach the gold ring blank to the back of the cardstock circle. Allow to dry and set.

VICTORIAN ROSE CUFFS

Ever since I was a kid, I've always loved using paper cutouts in my jewelry projects. I remember making painted and decoupaged cardboard jewelry for my mom; she would go nuts for it. I'm pretty sure she even wore a few pieces in public! With the invention of home copying machines, I don't have to use up all of my precious paper clippings for a project. I can copy them and use them as many times as I want!

WHAT YOU'LL NEED MOD PODGE HARD COAT ◻ METAL CUFF JEWELRY BRACELET ◻ PHOTOCOPY OF ROSES, OR ANY KIND OF FLOWER ◻ SEED PEARLS ◻ ADHESIVE GEMSTONES ◻ SMALL BITS OF LACE ◻ PAINTBRUSH ◻ SCISSORS

WHAT YOU'LL DO

1 Cut out the photocopied images of the flowers, making sure they will fit on the cuff.

2 Paint a layer of the Mod Podge Hard Coat on the cuff; then adhere the paper flower cutouts. Allow to dry.

3 Apply an additional coat of Mod Podge Hard Coat (A).

4 Using a generous amount of Mod Podge Hard Coat, decoupage the lace pieces to the cuff.

5 Add pearls with more Mod Podge Hard Coat and let the cuff dry.

6 Add strips of adhesive backed gems and loose gems over the rest of the cuff and around the edges.

7 Apply a final coat of Mod Podge Hard Coat and let dry.

GLITTER-ACCENT DENIM SHIRT

DESIGNER: **Stacie Grissom**

GLITTER-ACCENT DENIM SHIRT

Every closet needs the all-American wardrobe staple: a denim shirt. This fashion project adds a bit of glitz to the shirt that goes with everything.

WHAT YOU'LL NEED MOD PODGE FABRIC ■ PAINTBRUSH ■ GLITTER (COLOR OF CHOICE)
■ DENIM SHIRT

WHAT YOU'LL DO

1 Prepare the denim by brushing on a generous layer of Mod Podge Fabric on collar, cuffs, and pockets, working one section at a time.

2 Immediately sprinkle glitter on top of the wet Mod Podge Fabric (A). Keep flat and allow to dry.

3 Once the first layer of Mod Podge Fabric is dry, look for patches of glitter-free denim. Fill in patches with another layer of Mod Podge Fabric and glitter.

4 Allow initial layers of glitter and Mod Podge to dry completely, and then add another thin layer of Mod Podge Fabric to seal loose glitter in place (B). Repeat process for all decorated sections of shirt. Let dry to the touch before wearing.

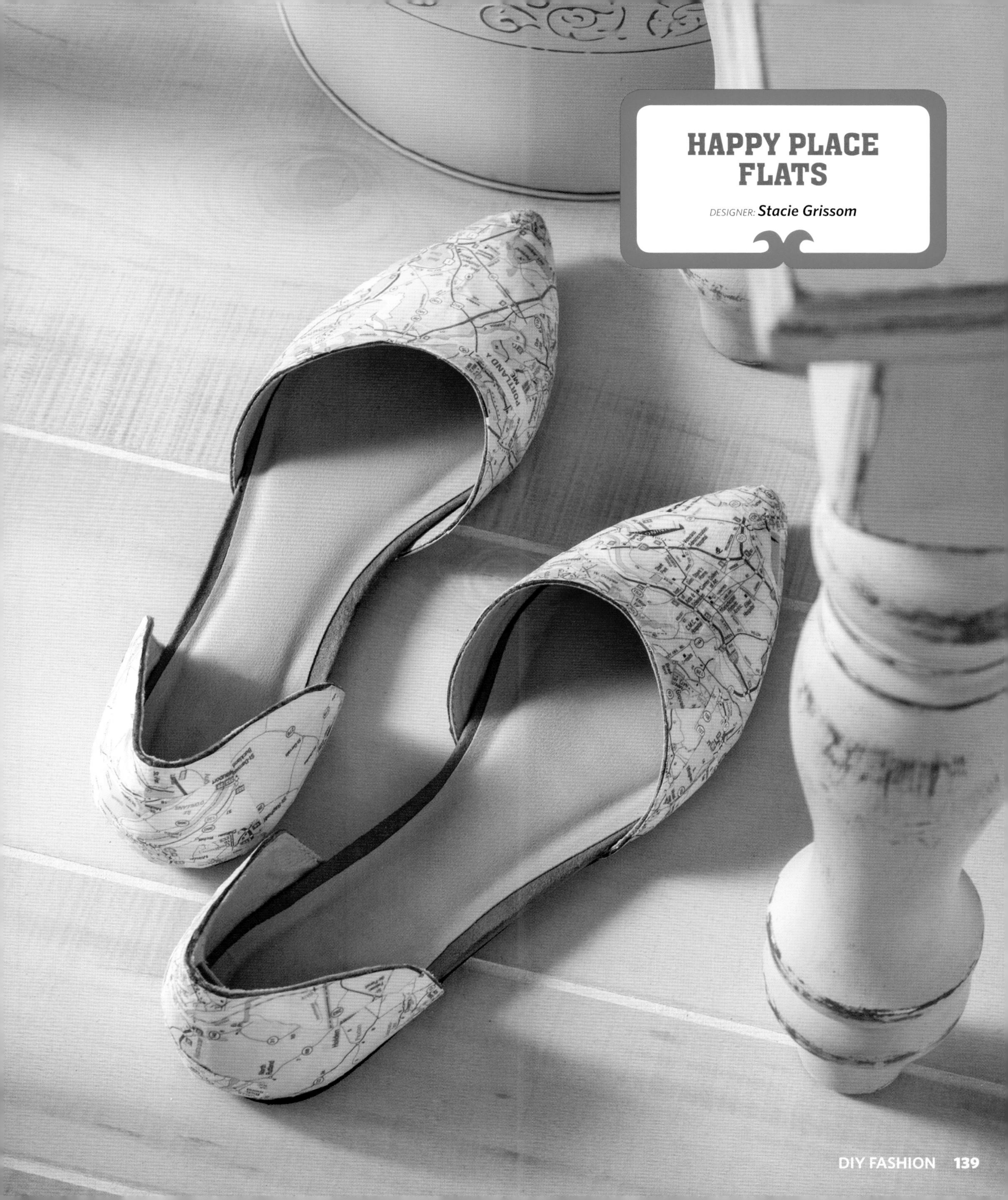

HAPPY PLACE FLATS

DESIGNER: ***Stacie Grissom***

HAPPY PLACE FLATS

When it comes to reminders of meaningful places and adventures, what better way to celebrate a special spot than on a pair of everyday flats? Keep warm memories of the past close in these comfy shoes—and better yet, make new memories and tromp around with new maps, in shoes for the effortless adventurer.

WHAT YOU'LL NEED MOD PODGE BASIC TOOL KIT (PAGE 18) ■ MOD PODGE FABRIC ■ FUN PAPER (SUCH AS MAPS) ■ PAIR OF FLAT SHOES ■ OPTIONAL MOD PODGE HARD COAT

WHAT YOU'LL DO

1 Cut paper into strips that will fit into the nooks and crannies of the shoes. Thin strips work well along edges, and wider strips work better in open areas.

2 Working a section of a shoe at a time, apply a generous layer of Mod Podge Fabric, and place the strips of paper on the shoes as you would a collage. It is best to start on the tricky spots and then move on to the easier places.

3 Continue applying Mod Podge Fabric and the paper strips until the shoe is covered and Mod Podge is dry. Repeat for second shoe.

4 Once the first layer of Mod Podge is dry, look for empty patches on the shoe. Fill open patches with another layer of Mod Podge Fabric and paper (A).

5 Allow Mod Podge to dry completely, and then add a thin layer of Mod Podge Fabric to seal everything in place. Let dry before using.

6 Optional—As added protection from the elements, an application of Mod Podge Hard Coat can be brushed over the entire surface of each shoe.

IT'S ART! MOD PODGE MIXED MEDIA

You can make layered collages of traditional art media, found objects, and imagery on a variety of functional and decorative surfaces.

THE BIG BOOK OF MOD PODGE®

STEAMPUNK ANGEL

DESIGNER: ***Carol Cook***

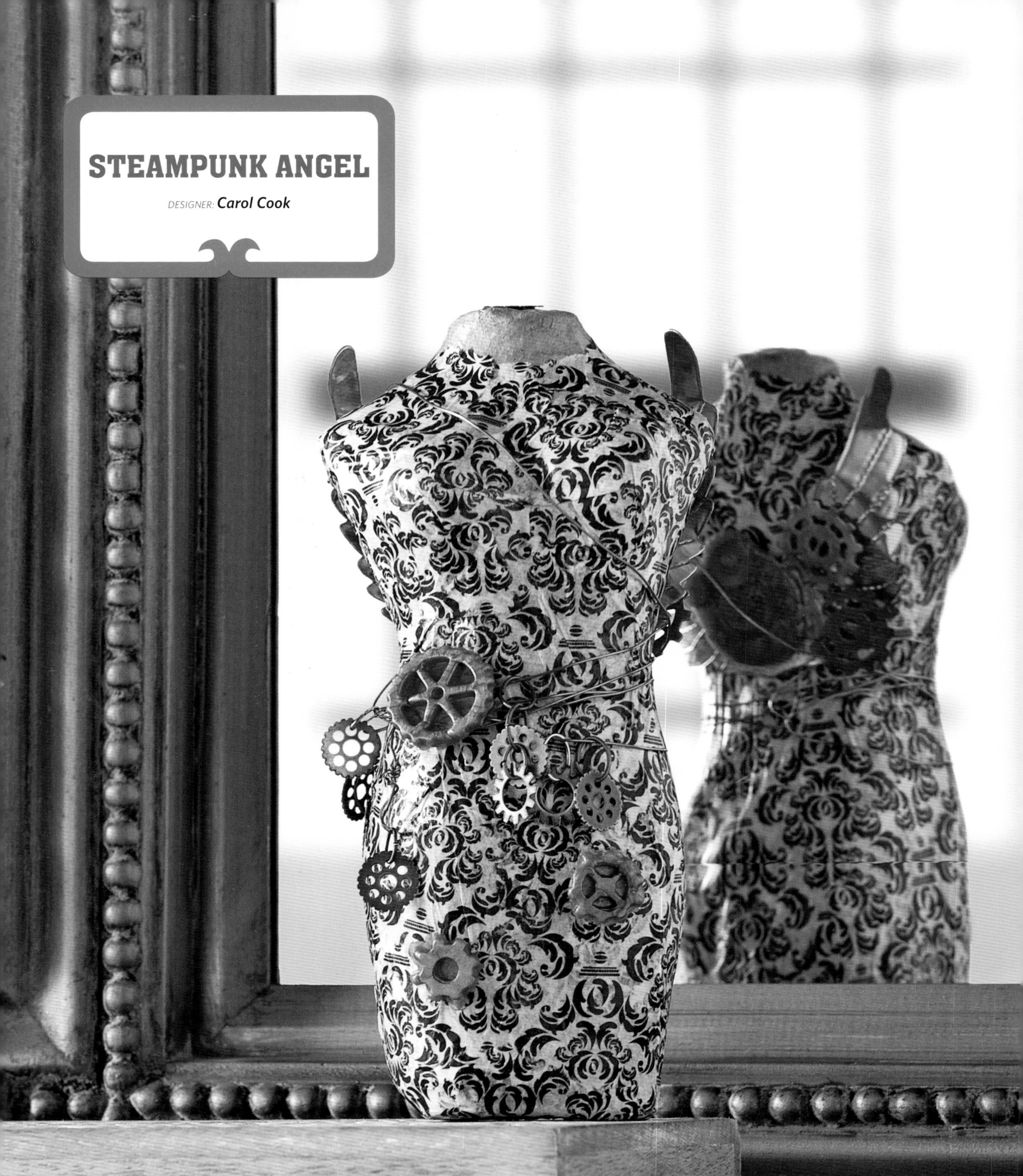

Grunge meets glam in this steampunk-inspired angel, which uses classic damask-print tissue paper and industrial elements of timepieces and gears.

WHAT YOU'LL NEED MOD PODGE BASIC TOOL KIT (PAGE 18) ■ MOD PODGE MATTE ■ MOD PODGE MOD MELTS, METALLIC GOLD ■ MOD PODGE MOD MOLD, INDUSTRIAL ■ FOLKART ACRYLIC PAINT, COPPER ■ 6-INCH (15 CM) TALL PAPIER-MÂCHÉ TORSO ■ SHEET OF 12 x 12-INCH (30.5 x 30.5 CM) PATTERNED TISSUE PAPER ■ METAL GEAR CHARMS ■ COPPER WIRE (ENOUGH TO WRAP AROUND PAPIER-MÂCHÉ TORSO A COUPLE OF TIMES) ■ DIE-CUT COPPER WINGS, TO FIT BACK OF TORSO ■ JEWELRY JUMP RINGS, ONE FOR EACH CHARM ■ MOD PODGE MOD MELTER ■ MOD PODGE WONDER GLUE

WHAT YOU'LL DO

1 Crinkle tissue paper and tear into random-sized pieces.

2 Working in small sections, apply Mod Podge Matte to torso. Cover with pieces of tissue paper (A). Allow to dry. Brush entire torso with additional coat of Mod Podge Matte. Let dry.

3 Create industrial gear embellishments using Mod Podge Mod Melter, Mod Podge Mod Melts, and Mod Podge Mod Mold. Apply light coat of FolkArt Acrylic Paint in Copper to Mod Podge Mod Melt embellishments. Let dry.

4 Glue wings to back of torso with hot Mod Podge Mod Melt. Wrap torso randomly with copper wire. Dab Mod Podge Wonder Glue or other strong glue to each end of wire to adhere wire ends to papier-mâché torso.

5 Attach gear charms to wire with jump rings.

6 Continue gluing using Mod Podge Wonder Glue to adhere Mod Podge Mod Melt gear embellishments and metal charm gears to torso.

A

GARDENING DOLL ALTERED BIRDHOUSE

DESIGNER: **Chris Williams**

She Realized It Was Her Time To Shine!

Time to shine! Combining my love of mixed media and garden art was an easy task for this project. Altering a birdhouse to a gardening doll is simple and fun step by step. Once created, you'll want to enjoy her indoors.

WHAT YOU'LL NEED   MOD PODGE BASIC TOOL KIT (PAGE 18)   ■   MOD PODGE MATTE   ■   FOLKART MULTI-SURFACE PAINT: PARCHMENT, PINK MELON, WICKER WHITE, AQUA, AND COFFEE LATTE   ■   SCALLOPED-ROOF WOOD BIRDHOUSE   ■   WOOD DOWEL (FOR LEGS)   ■   2 WOOD HALF EGGS (FOR FEET)   ■   5-INCH (12.7 CM) SQUARE WOOD PLAQUE (FOR BASE)   ■   WOOD NAPKIN RING (FOR NECK)   ■   2 ½-INCH (6.4 CM) WOOD BALL (FOR HEAD)   ■   2 WAGON WHEELS (FOR KNEES)   ■   ASSORTED SCRAPBOOK PAPERS   ■   SMALL STENCIL BRUSH   ■   MOD PODGE WONDER GLUE   ■   FLAT-BACK GEMS   ■   AQUA ORGANZA RIBBON   ■   CURLY DOLL HAIR   ■   18-GAUGE WIRE (FOR ARMS)   ■   SMALL FEATHERED BIRD (FOR HAT ORNAMENT)   ■   DOLL HAT   ■   MINI PAINT CAN OR SMALL TIN PAIL   ■   2-INCH (5 CM) STYROFOAM BALL   ■   LACE TRIM FOR DOLL'S SKIRT   ■   CROCHETED TRIM WITH HANGING BUTTONS (FOR SKIRT)   ■   PAPER BRADS OR PUSHPINS   ■   DIMENSIONAL ADHESIVE DOTS (OPTIONAL)   ■   DRILL AND DRILL BIT   ■   WOOD SAW   ■   TEMPLATES (PAGE 230)

WHAT YOU'LL DO

1 Begin by whittling or drilling two holes into the base of the square plaque and base of the birdhouse for doll's legs. Holes should be as large as diameter of dowel, and far enough apart to accommodate two half eggs next to each other for feet. Cut dowel to desired length for legs, but don't assemble these or other parts yet.

2 Paint dowels, wagon wheels (knees), half eggs, and wood ball (for face) skintone color by mixing a touch of FolkArt Multi-Surface Paint in Pink Melon with Wicker White. If desired, you can add a tiny touch of Coffee Latte. Allow to dry and reapply paint color.

3 Using FolkArt Multi-Surface Paint in Coffee Latte, paint two dot eyes and eyebrows on the wood ball. Add a tiny dot of Wicker White to the eyes to add sparkle. Paint a Pink Melon heart-shaped mouth and add a touch of blush to her cheeks.

TIP: *A neat way to paint blush is to stipple the color on using a stencil brush loaded with color, and then off-loaded to achieve an almost drybrush effect.*

4 Using FolkArt Multi-Surface Paint, paint Pink Melon on the outer edges of the napkin ring (it will become the neck), on the bird perch, and on the edges of the scalloped

sections of the birdhouse roof. Use Coffee Latte and Aqua for the routed edges of the square plaque. Color shoes on the wood eggs Aqua. Embellish shoes with Wicker White polka dots, using the handle end of paintbrush. Paint circular base of birdhouse Aqua. Color 2-inch (5 cm) Styrofoam ball Aqua. Let paint dry.

5 While paint is drying, begin cutting patterned scrapbook papers for all surfaces. See photo for guidance. The body of the birdhouse was decoupaged in 1-inch (2.5 cm) strips of coordinating papers. The birdhouse roof papers were cut following the shape of the wood scallop roof (the pattern is provided in the Template section of this book. Also prepare scrapbook paper edge for the wood square plaque and for around the metal pail.

6 Once all paper sections are cut, begin applying them to the surfaces, using Mod Podge Matte. Continue until all surfaces have been decoupaged. Let dry.

7 Cut rose flowers from one patterned paper and Mod Podge to the top of the wooden egg shoes.

8 Add a strip of paper to the center of the napkin ring using Mod Podge Matte.

GARDENING DOLL ALTERED BIRDHOUSE

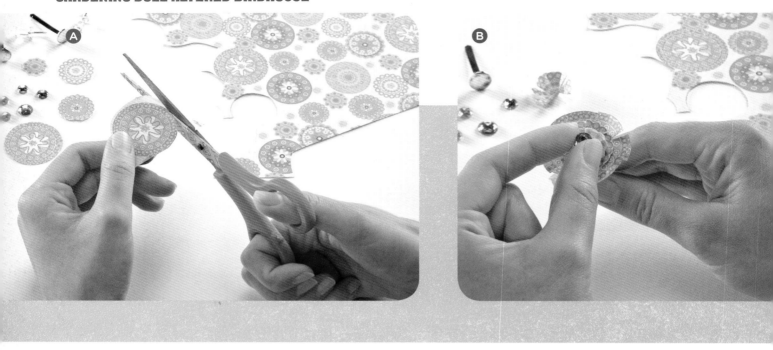

9 Once all surfaces have been decoupaged, apply an extra coat of Mod Podge Matte to the surfaces to seal and protect. Allow to dry.

10 Copy and cut the words "She Realized It Was Her Time to Shine" from white paper. Mod Podge to the roof as pictured. Allow to dry. Add a touch of FolkArt Multi-Surface Paint in Aqua to the edges of the white paper. When dry, brush a coat of Mod Podge Matte over the text.

11 Insert the painted Styrofoam ball into the small metal pail. Create paper flowers to add to the pail. To make flowers: cut circles of scrapbook paper in assorted sizes (A). Snip the edges of the circles, cutting toward the center (like making pie wedges), without cutting completely to the center. Layer paper circles with the largest on bottom and smallest circle on top, and hot-glue to a paper brad or pushpin. If a dimensional look is desired, add a dimensional adhesive dot between each pair of circles. Complete flower by hot-gluing a flat-back gem in the center (B). Push flowers into the painted Styrofoam ball.

12 Assemble gardening doll using Mod Podge Wonder Glue. Attach the wood dowels to the wood plaque base and attach wood egg shoes in front of the dowels. Thread painted wagon wheels onto dowels and affix middle of dowels as knees. Attach the birdhouse to the top of the dowels. Glue on the wood napkin ring at top of birdhouse to give doll a neck and then adhere the painted wood head. Allow adhesive to set before moving your altered birdhouse.

13 Continue embellishing your altered birdhouse by wrapping aqua organza ribbon over the 18-gauge wire; glue edges of ribbon together, creating sleeves. Wrap desired length of wire around the napkin ring neck, leaving equal lengths as arms. At the end, make loops of wire to resemble hands. Attach the metal pail in one hand and a paper flower in the other.

14 Cut assorted lengths of curly doll hair, and glue to head with hot glue or with a heavy white craft glue.

15 Glue a length of aqua organza ribbon around crown of hat and tie a bow. Glue small feathered bird to rim of hat, and glue hat on doll head.

16 Tie ribbon bows and glue to ankles. Cut and glue length of lace to wrap around birdhouse base, creating a skirt. Further embellish with a layer of button/crochet trim.

STACKED CRATE MIXED MEDIA BOOKSHELF

DESIGNER: ***Debbie Saenz***

STACKED CRATE MIXED MEDIA BOOKSHELF

My love for mixed media was the inspiration for this fun and whimsical bookshelf made from crates. While I was making this piece, my mind was soaring with so many ideas for the next one! By changing the paper designs and embellishments, there are so many possibilities of things to make—a dollhouse, a birdhouse, or even a schoolhouse! This would make the perfect conversation piece for any room.

WHAT YOU'LL NEED MOD PODGE FURNITURE SATIN ◼ FOLKART ACRYLIC PAINTS: APPLE RED AND LICORICE ◼ 3 WOOD CRATES ◼ BROWN WOOD STAIN ◼ PREMIUM GIFT WRAP (CONTINUOUS ROLL) ◼ WOOD SAW ◼ WOOD TRIM ◼ ⅝-INCH (1.6 CM) SQUARE WOOD DOWEL ◼ ⁷⁄₁₆-INCH (1.1 CM) WOOD DOWEL ◼ FOUR 2-INCH (5 CM) WOOD BALL KNOBS (FOR FEET) ◼ 6 COORDINATING SCRAPBOOK PAPERS, 12 x 12 INCHES (30.5 x 30.5 CM) EACH ◼ DISTRESSING INK AND DENSE FOAM COSMETIC SPONGE ◼ NAILS ◼ WOOD GLUE ◼ WOOD FILLER ◼ BRACKETS ◼ RED RIBBON, WIDTH OF SHELF FRONT, AND AS LONG AS 2 SHELVES ◼ 2 FABRIC MEASURING TAPES ◼ MOD PODGE WONDER GLUE ◼ TWO 5-INCH (12.7 CM) WOOD NUMBERS: 1 AND 6 ◼ TWO 5-INCH (12.7 CM) WOOD LETTERS: S AND W ◼ 3-INCH (7.6 CM) WOOD CIRCLE ◼ 3 LARGE RED BRADS, FOR ATTACHING NUMERALS TO FRONT OF SHELF ◼ DECORATIVE EMBELLISHMENT FOR ROOF ◼ DECORATIVE EMBELLISHMENT FOR SIDE ◼ 9 OLD TICKETS (FROM SHOWS, MOVIES, ETC.) ◼ FINE-GRIT SANDPAPER

WHAT YOU'LL DO

1 Remove the side slats from two crates (middle and top crates for shelf), and set aside for roof. Remove the bottoms from three crates; set aside to decoupage.

2 Cut eight wood slats into 14-inch (36 cm) pieces (for roof). Cut wood dowels into 9⅜-inch (23.8 cm) pieces. Cut wood trim into two pieces, one 38 inches (96.5 cm) and one 53 inches (134.6 cm).

3 Stain the insides of crates with brown stain. Using FolkArt Acrylic Paint in Apple Red, paint the wood trim, the wood ball knobs (for feet), the rough sides and edges of roof slats, and the square and round dowels. Paint edges of letters, numbers, and circle in FolkArt Acrylic paint in Licorice.

4 Apply gift wrap to smooth side of each slat for back of bookshelf with Mod Podge Furniture Satin, and smooth out bubbles. Apply gift wrap to exterior sides of each crate with Mod Podge Furniture Satin, smoothing out bubbles.

When dry, sand off all extra paper that extends beyond the edges with sandpaper. Distress edges with distressing ink. Seal with two or more coats of Mod Podge Furniture Satin, allowing shelf to dry between coats.

5 Use nails and wood glue to attach slats to bottom of each crate with designs facing up (will be back of bookshelf). Stack crates, using wood glue between crates. Reinforce by driving nails at an angle on insides of crates. Use four metal brackets (on the back of shelf) to connect crates for extra support.

6 Nail (reinforce with wood glue) roof slats (smooth sides facing up) evenly spaced across square wood dowel at a 45-degree angle to construct roof. Align roof evenly on the top crate, and nail to attach (reinforce with wood glue) at an angle. Sink nails into wood and fill holes with wood filler. Allow to dry; then sand smooth.

STACKED CRATE MIXED MEDIA BOOKSHELF

7 Cut a decorative paper to the size of the roof slats and adhere decorative papers to roof slats (you will have a seam) with Mod Podge Furniture Satin. When dry, sand off all extra paper that extends beyond edges with sandpaper (A). Distress edges with distressing ink. Distress edges of tickets with distressing ink and adhere over seam on right side of roof. Seal roof with two or more coats of Mod Podge Furniture Satin, allowing it to dry between coats.

8 Attach red ribbon to front of edge top shelf (right under roof) and to lower edge of bottom shelf with Mod Podge Wonder Glue. With same glue, attach fabric measuring tapes to front edges of middle shelf and along left side of bookshelf. Distress edges of remaining tickets with distressing ink, and adhere over left side of shelf where crates meet. Seal with a coat of Mod Podge Furniture Satin.

9 Adhere decorative papers to numbers, letters, and wood circle with Mod Podge Furniture Satin. Sand off excess paper from edges. Distress edges with distressing ink. Seal with two or more coats of Mod Podge Furniture Satin, allowing it to dry between coats. Drill three holes into the number 1. Attach brads in holes.

10 Glue numbers to top left front of bookshelf. Glue letters to right side of bookshelf. Attach embellishment to circle and glue to left side of bookshelf. To antique wood trim, paint with wood stain and wipe off. Glue wood trim to side edges of front of bookshelf. Glue ball feet to bottom of bookshelf with wood glue. Let everything dry before using shelf.

ENJOY THE RIDE
PALLET ART

DESIGNER: *Kirsten Jones*

Reclaimed pallets are such a popular way to decorate! Create a bold piece of art, using your favorite quote, some patterned papers, and a recycled pallet or skid.

WHAT YOU'LL NEED MOD PODGE SATIN ▪ FOLKART ACRYLIC PAINTS: STEEL GRAY, MIDNIGHT, SKY BLUE, AND WICKER WHITE ▪ PAINTBRUSHES ▪ RECLAIMED WOODEN PALLET ▪ 5 OR 6 ASSORTED PATTERNED SCRAPBOOK PAPERS ▪ POSTER ART (ON MODEL, BICYCLES) ▪ 5-INCH (12.7 CM) WOOD LETTERS (ON PROJECT, **DREAM**) ▪ 6-INCH (15.2 CM) PRESSED BOARD WORD (ON MODEL, "LIVE") ▪ LARGE WOOD ARROW ▪ SMALL WOOD HEART ▪ WOOD EMBELLISHMENTS (WINGS AND CARVED TILES) ▪ WOOD GLUE ▪ SANDPAPER ▪ RAGS ▪ SCISSORS ▪ PENCIL

WHAT YOU'LL DO

1 Sand and dust pallet so that it is clean and ready to craft on.

2 Cut poster art to fit one side of pallet. Roughly tear the edges to create a distressed look for the poster. Cut the poster to fit the wood that is unique to your pallet. (The project pallet had two open sections, so I cut my bicycle poster into two sections.) Using Mod Podge Satin, apply the poster to the pallet.

3 Roughly rip the scrapbook papers to be about ½ inch (1.3 cm) narrower than the width of each slat of the pallet you plan to decorate (A). Rip each paper pattern the length of the wood slat to be decorated and, using Mod Podge Satin, apply each paper to the pallet (B). Let all papers dry.

4 Paint DREAM with FolkArt Acrylic Paint in Sky Blue and let dry. Use FolkArt Acrylic Paint in Midnight to paint the letters "Live," and let dry. Using the letters of "Live" as patterns, trace them onto the scrapbook paper and cut out. Using Mod Podge Satin, apply paper to the letters, and let dry.

5 Paint the large arrow with two coats of FolkArt Acrylic Paint in Steel Gray. Let dry. Sand to create distressed look on the arrow.

6 Using the wood heart as a pattern, trace around the heart on scrapbook paper; then cut out. Apply paper to the wood heart with Mod Podge Satin. Let dry.

7 Mix 1 part FolkArt Acrylic Paint in Wicker White with 1 part water. Wash the wood tiles and small wood wings, creating a whitewashed look. Let dry.

8 Using sandpaper, sand the edges of the papers and of the poster design. This will distress the edges even more and make the art and paper look like parts of the pallet.

9 Glue everything onto your pallet with wood glue and let dry for 12 hours.

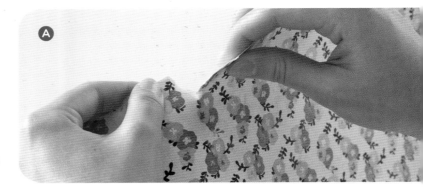

JEWELRY-HOLDING HEAD FORM

DESIGNER: **Sherrie Ragsdale**

Add a vintage flare to the bedroom with this vintage-styled head form jewelry holder.

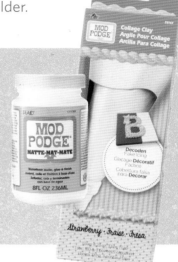

WHAT YOU'LL NEED   MOD PODGE BASIC TOOL KIT (PAGE 18)   ▢   MOD PODGE MATTE   ▢
MOD PODGE SHEER COLOR, PINK   ▢   LINER BRUSH   ▢   MOD PODGE MOD MOLDS, ROYAL ICON   ▢
MOD PODGE MOD MELTER   ▢   MOD PODGE MOD MELT, MILK GLASS WHITE   ▢   MOD PODGE COLLAGE
CLAY, STRAWBERRY PINK   ▢   FOLKART ACRYLIC PAINTS: VINTAGE WHITE, PEARL WHITE, AND LICORICE
▢   OLD BOOK PAGES   ▢   STYROFOAM HEAD WIG HOLDER   ▢   CHANDELIER LAMPSHADE   ▢   STRONG
WIRE CUTTERS   ▢   WIRE: SECTIONS 5–11 INCHES (12.7-27.9 CM) LONG   ▢   PLIERS   ▢   ROLL OF TWINE   ▢
¾-INCH-WIDE (1.9 CM) LACE   ▢   WHITE PEARLS   ▢   LARGE PINK GEMS   ▢   SMALL PINK GEMS   ▢   PINK
GLASS BEADS   ▢   LARGE PINK RESIN PENDANT   ▢   WOODEN PEDESTAL   ▢   SANDPAPER

WHAT YOU'LL DO

1 Cut squares from pages of an old book. Mod Podge paper squares onto the Styrofoam wig head with Mod Podge Matte, overlapping to cover whole head. Using FolkArt Acrylic Paint in Vintage White, paint the base of head, and lightly drybrush the rest of the head Vintage White. Allow to dry.

2 Lightly brush Mod Podge Sheer Color Pink over each cheek, making it darker in some places than in others. Paint lips Mod Podge Sheer Color Pink, using a liner brush.

3 For the crown, cut away the central ring support that rests on the light bulb from the lampshade, using wire cutters. Remove fabric from shade. Cut five 11-inch-long (28 cm) pieces of wire. Fold over one end of wire about 1½ inches (3.8 cm) and hook to narrowest circle of the shade, where the vertical wire support meets the rim of shade. Bend the folded wire around the smaller wire circle of the lampshade (A). Tie the twine around the piece of wire and the vertical wire support and begin wrapping the wire around all the way to end of the wire, past the widest rim of the shade (B). Use hot glue to secure the twine at the ends. Curl the wire end with the pliers (C). Repeat for the other 4 wires. Wrap twine around the bottom and top rim of the shade. Use Mod Podge Mod Melter and Mod Podge Mod Melt to secure ends.

4 Wrap twine around the entire bottom (widest part) of lampshade frame, going up 1½ inches (3.8 cm). Hot-glue to secure. Glue lace around the middle of the wrapped twine. Create Mod Podge Mod Mold embellishments; then paint using FolkArt Acrylic Paint in Pearl White. Glue Mod Mold embellishments in place. Refer to the photo at the beginning of this project.

5 Using the star tip of the Mod Podge Collage Clay Strawberry Pink, make stars in the center of one of the royal icons and add a white pearl in the center.

Ⓐ

JEWELRY-HOLDING HEAD FORM

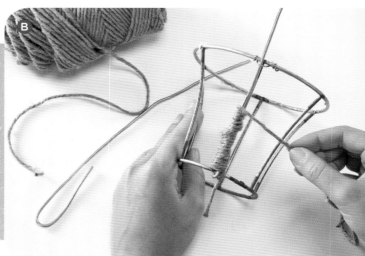

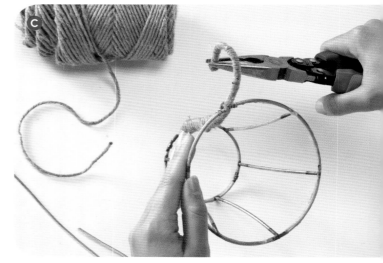

6 Glue large pink gems around base of crown, on top of wrapped twine as shown in the opening photo. Add the small row of pink gems at the bottom and in between the fleurs de lis.

7 To secure the crown to the head, cut four 2-inch (5 cm) pieces of wire and fold. Push the folded wire into the head, grabbing the base wire of lampshade as you go. Add hot melt to the ends of the wire before inserting to add extra security.

8 Glue lace around the bottom of the neck. Add Mod Podge Collage Clay Strawberry Pink stars on top of the lace and then put in pink glass beads (D).

9 Add a Mod Podge Collage Clay Strawberry Pink star to the center of a large pink resin pendant flower and then push in a pearl. Thread twine through to make a necklace and then tie in a bow.

10 Paint the pedestal using FolkArt Acrylic Paint in Licorice. Allow to dry; then drybrush with FolkArt Acrylic Paint in Vintage White. Allow to dry; then sand to distress. Wipe clean.

11 Add Mod Podge Collage Clay Strawberry Pink stars to the base of the pedestal and around the edge. Push in pearls, pink gems, glass beads, and heart Mod Podge Mod Mold embellishments painted with FolkArt Acrylic Paint in Vintage White.

12 Using the Mod Podge Mod Melter, glue the head to the pedestal. Let everything dry to the touch before use.

TYPOGRAPHY WALL ART (RECYCLED CABINET DOOR)

Create your own mid-century graphic design wall art.

WHAT YOU'LL NEED MOD PODGE HARD COAT ☐ MOD PODGE MOD MELTER ☐ MOD PODGE MOD MELTS: BLUE, RED, AND MILK GLASS WHITE ☐ MOD PODGE COLLAGE CLAY, VANILLA WHITE ☐ MOD PODGE MOD MOLDS: ALPHABET, GEMS, AND TRINKETS ☐ CABINET DOOR ☐ RED GLITTER ☐ SMALL FLAT BRUSH ☐ PICTURE WIRE WITH HOOKS

WHAT YOU'LL DO

1 Insert Mod Podge Blue Mod Melt into Mod Podge Mod Melter and fill Mod Podge Alphabet Mod Mold. Remove those letters when cool and fill Mod Mold Alphabet letters L-O-V-E with Mod Podge Red Mod Melt. Fill one heart with Mod Podge Red Mod Melt. Remove when cool.

2 Mix a little red glitter with Mod Podge Hard Coat. Brush glitter mixture onto heart Mod Podge Mod Mold embellishment. Let dry.

3 Place Mod Podge Mod Mold alphabet embellishments on cabinet to determine placement and quantity. Continue creating additional blue letters to fill space.

4 For the border, use Mod Podge Gems Mod Mold to make pearl-shaped strand with the Mod Podge Milk Glass White Mod Melt. Create enough Mod Podge Mod Mold pearl strand embellishments to border the cabinet door panel.

5 Apply Mod Podge Collage Clay Vanilla White in the center of the cabinet door (A). Using a palette knife, smooth the application of Mod Podge Collage Clay

Vanilla White, as you would icing a cake (B). Next, insert blue letter embellishments randomly in the first four horizontal rows of Mod Podge Collage Clay. Then embed the red L-O-V-E letters and the red glittered heart. Continue applying Mod Podge Collage Clay Vanilla White to the cabinet panel and, while it is still wet, embed the remaining blue Mod Podge Mod Mold alphabet embellishments (C).

6 Create a border trim on the door using the pearl strand Mod Podge embellishments. Allow to dry.

7 Add picture wire to the back of the wall art, and hang.

B

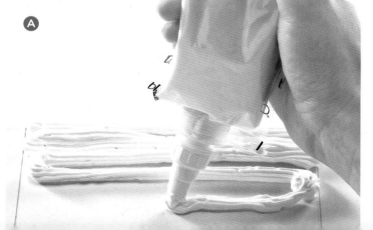
A

C

FURNITURE FACELIFTS

Everyone is doing it . . . thrifting and upcycling used furniture is the craze. Every DIY enthusiast will love giving their hands a try at decoupaging and repurposing, bringing new life to ordinary furniture.

THE BIG BOOK OF MOD PODGE®

STAMPED WITH LOVE JEWELRY BOX

DESIGNER: *Candie Cooper*

A little Mod Podge, a little paint, and a few old postage stamps will transform an old throwaway jewelry box into a piece of art everyone will want to display!

WHAT YOU'LL NEED MOD PODGE BASIC TOOL KIT (PAGE 18) ▪ MOD PODGE FURNITURE GLOSS ▪ FOLKART ACRYLIC PAINTS: LICORICE, METALLIC PURE GOLD ▪ RECYCLED JEWELRY BOX ▪ TACK CLOTH OR RAG ▪ STIFF BRISTLE BRUSH ▪ POSTAGE STAMPS ▪ BRASS FLAT-BACK EMBELLISHMENTS ▪ PRINTED BURLAP ▪ PAPER

WHAT YOU'LL DO

1 Sand the jewelry box surface lightly to add tooth for the paint to adhere.

2 Wipe the jewelry box clean with a damp cloth.

3 Paint the surface of the box and drawer fronts using FolkArt Acrylic Paint in Licorice.

4 Drybrush the jewelry box with FolkArt Acrylic Paint in Metallic Pure Gold, using a stiff bristle brush. To drybrush, dip the bristles lightly in the paint, wipe off excess onto paper towel, and then brush over the box to create a textured effect (A).

5 Lay the postage stamps in desired pattern on top of the jewelry box (B). Use Mod Podge Furniture Gloss to adhere them to the box top and other desired areas.

6 Seal the entire box with Mod Podge Furniture Gloss.

7 Embellish the edge of the box top with brass flat-back embellishments, adhered with Mod Podge Furniture Gloss.

8 Cut burlap pieces to fit the inside of the jewelry box sections. Brush a coat of Mod Podge Furniture Gloss on each interior piece and apply cut burlap (C). Areas of the inside of the box that can't be covered with burlap can be painted with FolkArt Acrylic Paints.

Textured scrapbook papers and Mod Podge Furniture are the perfect combination for creating faux inlaid tabletops and furniture. The papers are available in a variety of textures. Look for papers with wood grain, marbled paint, and even cork designs at your local craft shop. This project uses faux cork scrapbook paper.

WHAT YOU'LL NEED MOD PODGE BASIC TOOL KIT (PAGE 18) ☐ MOD PODGE FURNITURE SATIN ☐ MOD PODGE CRAFT MAT ☐ BOWL FOR TRACING ☐ SHEET OF CARDSTOCK SCRAPBOOK PAPER, 12 x 12 INCHES (30.5 x 30.5 CM) ☐ 16 SHEETS FAUX CORK SCRAPBOOK PAPER, 12 x 12 INCHES (30.5 x 30.5 CM) EACH ☐ SHEET OF ORANGE SCRAPBOOK PAPER, 12 x 12 INCHES (30.5 x 30.5 CM) ☐ FOAM APPLICATOR ☐ CIRCLE PUNCH ☐ PARSONS TABLE TO BE DECORATED (COLOR OF CHOICE) ☐ TEMPLATE (PAGE 229)

WHAT YOU'LL DO

1 Use pattern provided in Template section or create your own template by tracing the bowl onto the cardstock scrapbook paper. Cut out the circle. Fold the circle in half and then in half again. Leaving the paper folded in quarters, place the edge of the bowl over the curved edge of the folded paper with its curve facing opposite to the curved edge of the paper, with the rim of the bowl touching the corners of the paper next to the folds on curve ends. This will create the curved edge of the template. Cut away the football-shaped part of the folded paper through all four layers, along the traced line.

2 Open the template. Trace the template onto the faux cork paper and cut out, creating as many faux cork pattern pieces as needed for the size of your project surface (A). Cut a few of the cork shapes in half down the center.

FAUX CORK INLAY TABLE

3 Punch circles from the orange paper (B). Cut a few in half down the center.

4 Layout the design plan on the top of the table top to be decorated. Use the sample photo in the book as a design guide. Find the center of the table and begin there, working toward the edges.

5 Place a cork shape right-side down on the craft mat.

6 Apply Mod Podge Furniture Satin to the back of the cork shape with a foam applicator. Do this one piece at a time.

7 Apply the cork shapes on the tabletop, one piece at a time. Press with your fingers to remove any air bubbles.

8 Topcoat the strips with Mod Podge Furniture Satin.

9 Continue doing steps 5–7 until the entire tabletop is covered. Apply a second topcoat to add additional protection to your tabletop. Allow to dry for 4 hours.

10 Apply Mod Podge Furniture Satin to the back of the orange circles. Place onto the table where the cork shapes intersect. Topcoat with a layer of Mod Podge Furniture Satin.

11 Apply Mod Podge Furniture Satin over the entire tabletop. Allow to dry overnight.

BONUS PROJECT

RECYCLED PARTY TRAY

Recycling is all about looking for the next way something can be used. This retro flower-inspired party tray began as a simple pizza pan.

WHAT YOU'LL NEED MOD PODGE BASIC TOOL KIT (PAGE 18) ▪ MOD PODGE FURNITURE SATIN ▪ MOD PODGE CRAFT MAT ▪ PIZZA PAN ▪ ORANGE SPRAY PAINT ▪ SHEET OF TURQUOISE SCRAPBOOK PAPER, 12 x 12 INCHES (30.5 x 30.5 CM) ▪ SHEET OF FAUX CORK SCRAPBOOK PAPER, 12 x 12 INCHES (30.45 x 30.5 CM) ▪ SCALLOPED CIRCLE PUNCH (OPTIONAL) ▪ FOAM BRUSH (FOR APPLYING MOD PODGE) ▪ SCISSORS

WHAT YOU'LL DO

1 Paint the pizza pan with orange spray paint. Be sure to work outdoors or in a well-ventilated space. Allow to dry.

2 Punch or cut 19 small circles from the turquoise paper for petals and 5 from the faux cork paper for flower centers.

3 Cut three narrow strips from the faux cork paper for flower stems. Following the photo shown, plan your flower design. Lightly mark flower centers on tray for guidance, if needed.

4 Place the circles and strips right-side down on the craft mat.

5 Apply Mod Podge Furniture Satin to the backs of the strips of paper, using a foam brush.

6 Apply the strips to the tray. Use the sample design for placement inspiration. Press with your fingers to remove any air bubbles.

7 Topcoat the strips with more Mod Podge Furniture Satin.

8 Apply Mod Podge Furniture Satin to the backs of the turquoise circles, one at a time. Place turquoise circles onto the tray in small clusters to imitate petals of flowers. Apply more Mod Podge Furniture Satin to the top and smooth with your fingers to remove any air bubbles. Add the cork circles to the centers of the petal groups, and topcoat with a layer of Mod Podge Furniture Satin.

9 Apply Mod Podge Furniture Satin over the entire tray. Allow to dry, and topcoat with a second layer of Mod Podge Furniture Satin for additional protection.

UPCYCLED PEDESTAL KITCHEN TABLE

DESIGNER: **Julie Lewis**

When it comes to what is personal, I always strive to be different and unique. Here is a way to turn an ordinary kitchen table into a singular work of art.

WHAT YOU'LL NEED MOD PODGE BASIC TOOL KIT (PAGE 18) ■ MOD PODGE FURNITURE SATIN ■ MOD PODGE 4-INCH (10 CM) BRUSH APPLICATOR ■ FOLKART MULTI-SURFACE PAINT: APPLE RED, PINK MELON, AND WICKER WHITE ■ FOLKART CHALKBOARD PAINT, BLACK ■ PEDESTAL KITCHEN TABLE ■ MULTIPLE COLOR PHOTOCOPIES OF SCRAPBOOK PAPER FOR TABLETOP (CHOOSE BASED ON PERSONAL PREFERENCE) ■ PAINTER'S TAPE ■ STENCIL ■ STENCIL BRUSH ■ LIFE SIZE PHOTOCOPIES OF PLATES AND SILVERWARE (ONE FOR EACH PLACE SETTING) ■ CHALK ■ WAXED PAPER

WHAT YOU'LL DO

1 Make as many photocopies of the desired scrapbook paper as necessary to cover the entire tabletop, with patterns matched if desired. Starting in the center of the table, brush Mod Podge Furniture Satin onto surface; then place one photocopy over prepared Mod Podge area. Cover with waxed paper and smooth with Mod Podge Squeegee. Repeat process, lining up papers to match desired pattern, if there is one, until entire surface of table is covered. Let dry 20 minutes and seal with additional coats of Mod Podge Furniture Satin.

2 Measure and tape off two rectangles 15 x 11 inches (38.1 x 28 cm) each, which will serve as a placemat. Apply FolkArt Multi-Surface Paint in Pink Melon. Let dry. Tape off a 3-inch (7.6 cm) border along left side of rectangle and paint a "napkin" border using FolkArt Multi-Surface Paint in Apple Red. Let dry. Place stencil over dark red border and stencil Pink Melon. Remove all tape.

3 From the photocopies of plates and silverware pieces, cut out elements you want to use (A). Apply Mod Podge Furniture Satin to back of paper and place on table as shown in photo. Cover with waxed paper and smooth out with Mod Podge Squeegee. When dry, seal tabletop again with Mod Podge Furniture Satin.

4 Paint desired sections such as pedestal and sections of base with FolkArt Chalkboard Paint in Black. When dry, condition by rubbing the side of a piece of chalk over surface, and wipe with paper towel.

5 Paint remaining sections of pedestal with FolkArt Multi-Surface Paint in Apple Red and Wicker White.

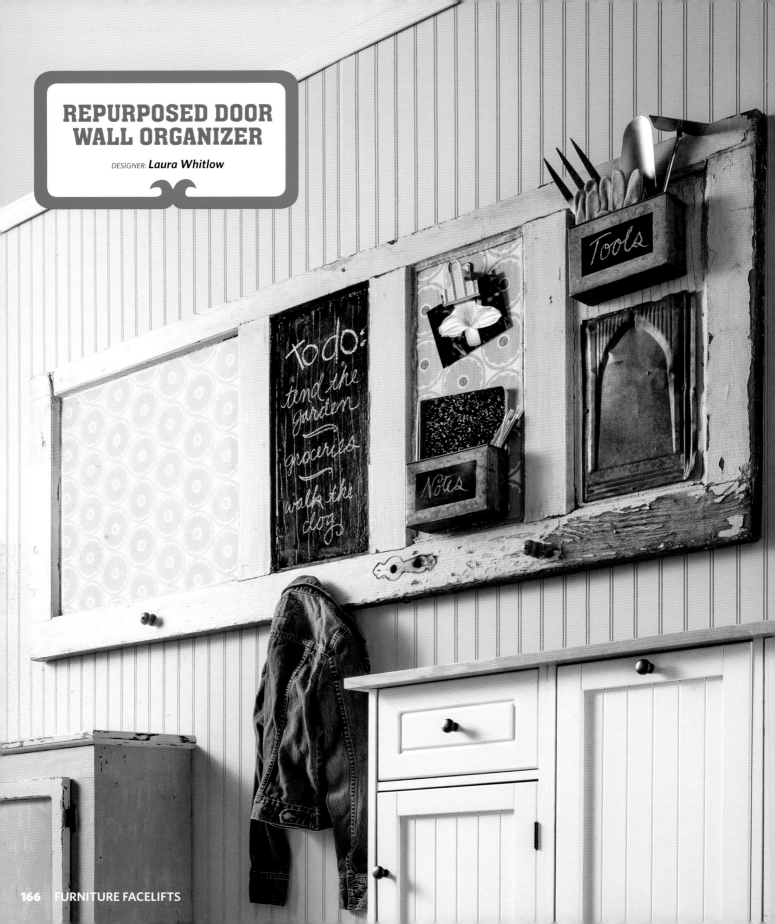

REPURPOSED DOOR WALL ORGANIZER

DESIGNER: **Laura Whitlow**

To do:
tend the
garden
groceries
walk the
dog

Tools

Notes

There is joy to be found when you can turn something old into something new and purposeful. Every active household needs an organizational board, so here is an example of repurposing an old door to make a family message center.

WHAT YOU'LL NEED MOD PODGE BASIC TOOL KIT (PAGE 18) ▢ MOD PODGE FURNITURE GLOSS ▢ FOLKART CHALKBOARD PAINT, BLACK ▢ DOOR WITH GLASS WINDOW AND WOOD PANELS (CAN BE OLD OR NEW, DEPENDING ON LOOK DESIRED) ▢ FLAT METAL OR WOODEN BOXES THAT CAN BE ATTACHED TO DOOR TO HOLD PENCILS, TOOLS, CHALK, ETC. ▢ SCREWS TO ATTACH BOXES AND HOOKS TO DOOR ▢ SCREWDRIVER ▢ COAT HOOKS OR KNOBS FOR HANGING THINGS ON DOOR ▢ OLD SHEETS OF TIN FOR DECORATION (OPTIONAL) ▢ WHITE CHALK ▢ FABRIC FOR COVERING SECTIONS OF DOOR ▢ MAGNETS ▢ MISCELLANEOUS ACCENTS, SUCH AS DECORATIVE BRAID (DEPENDING ON STYLE AND TASTE) ▢ HOT GLUE GUN AND GLUE STICKS

WHAT YOU'LL DO

1. Cut fabric to size using the glass panels on the door as a guide.

2. Decoupage the fabric onto what will become the backside of the glass parts of the door (will face the wall), using Mod Podge Furniture Gloss. The front side of the glass can be used as a dry-erase board.

3. Apply FolkArt Chalkboard Paint in Black to one wood panel of the door. Allow to dry and reapply an additional coat of chalkboard paint. Allow to dry. Condition the painted chalkboard surface before writing a message or note on the door. To condition the chalkboard surface, rub the side of a white chalk stick over the entire painted area; wipe away chalk dust with a damp paper towel.

4. Decoupage fabric on another wood panel of the door to balance the overall look. Using hot glue gun, add decorative braid around edges of panels (A).

5. Using screws and a screwdriver, attach metal or wood boxes, sheet of tin, and any other chosen accents directly to door.

6. Using screws and screwdriver, attach hooks or knobs to bottom of door to hold keys, dog leashes, scarves, etc. Colorful decorative drawer pulls can be used as hooks.

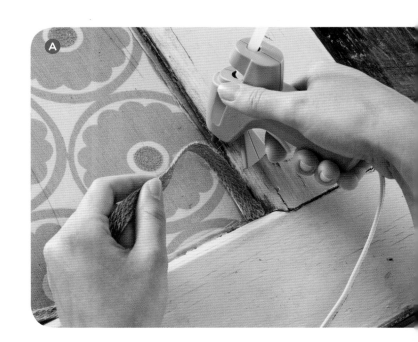

DECOUPAGED FABRIC HEADBOARD

DESIGNER: **Laura Whitlow**

Decoupaged fabric is a delightful surprise that works so well in a bedroom. Customizing a headboard is the perfect DIY project to enhance as well as coordinate with bed linens, and is so easy to do!

WHAT YOU'LL NEED MOD PODGE FURNITURE GLOSS ▪ HEADBOARD ▪ PAINT (COLOR OF YOUR CHOICE TO COORDINATE WITH CHOSEN FABRIC) ▪ PAINTBRUSH TO PAINT HEADBOARD ▪ SANDER ▪ 80-GRIT SANDPAPER ▪ FABRIC OF CHOICE ▪ SCISSORS ▪ MEASURING TAPE ▪ BRAIDED TRIM TO OUTLINE FABRIC PANELS (CHOOSE A TRIM THAT COORDINATES WITH THE FABRIC) ▪ HOT GLUE GUN AND GLUE STICKS

WHAT YOU'LL DO

1 Using paintbrush, apply paint to headboard. Just choose a color and start painting!

2 When headboard is dry, distress with electric sander and 80-grit sandpaper to achieve vintage look. Just hit all the edges to remove a little paint where desired.

3 Determine the areas where you desire fabric. Measure and then cut fabric to fit those areas being covered. This crafted headboard had inset areas, so it was easy to decide where to add the fabric accents.

4 Working a section at a time, brush a coat of Mod Podge Furniture Gloss onto the headboard. Press fabric to the headboard and smooth in place, working from the center out, releasing any caught air bubbles, and stretching fabric to remove any wrinkles. Allow to dry.

5 Once fabric is smooth and in place, brush another coat of Mod Podge Furniture Gloss over the fabric to seal and protect (A). Repeat for any other headboard sections where you decoupaged fabric. Allow to dry.

6 When Mod Podge is dry, use hot glue gun to adhere fabric braided trim around edges of fabric (B). This headboard is enhanced with burlap gimp as the trim. Adding the trim gives this project a polished look and hides any uneven fabric edges.

CLOSET DOOR ROOM DIVIDER

DESIGNER: **Laura Whitlow**

When upcycling a project surface, be creative! Not always is a project surface intended to be perfect. Sometimes it is best to get a little messy, leave a few wrinkles, sand to distress, and antique the project to create a time-worn aged or vintage feel.

WHAT YOU'LL NEED MOD PODGE BASIC TOOL KIT (PAGE 18) ◼ MOD PODGE FURNITURE SATIN ◼ TWO SETS OF BIFOLD CLOSET DOORS ◼ PAINT (COLOR OF CHOICE) ◼ SANDER ◼ 80-GRIT SANDPAPER ◼ SCRAPBOOK PAPER TO COVER SOME DOOR PANELS (COLORS COORDINATING WITH PAINT) ◼ DARK WALNUT FURNITURE WAX ◼ HINGES (TO JOIN 2 SECTIONS OF DOOR) ◼ DRILL AND DRILL BIT ◼ SCREWS ◼ SCREWDRIVER ◼ RAGS

WHAT YOU'LL DO

1. Paint bifold closet doors, front and back, using your color of choice. Allow to dry.

2. When thoroughly dry, distress edges of doors with sander and 80-grit sandpaper to achieve a rustic, aged look.

3. Measure and cut scrapbook paper to fit areas to be covered.

4. Apply Mod Podge Furniture Satin to door surface where scrapbook paper will go, as well as to wrong side of paper. Position paper where desired and apply to door. Smooth paper from center toward edges to release air bubbles and excess Mod Podge. (If desired, smooth wrinkles out of the paper. However this rustic project was created purposefully with paper wrinkles.) Allow to dry. Apply paper to both sides of the bifold closet doors where desired.

5. When completely dry, further enhance the worn, aged look by sanding the raised bumps and/or winkles in the paper (A).

6. Apply a topcoat of Mod Podge Furniture Satin to the bifold closet doors. Let dry.

7. Lightly apply dark walnut furniture wax to entire door, including decoupaged surfaces. The wax will further spotlight any irregularities and provide a wonderful rustic look (B).

8. Using hinges, drill, screws, and screwdriver, attach the sets of bifold doors to each other to complete the screen.

FRENCH GRAPHICS END TABLE

DESIGNER: **Laura Whitlow**

It is very gratifying to upcycle an old piece of furniture or a thrift store find. With a little paper and Mod Podge, any designer look is possible!

WHAT YOU'LL NEED MOD PODGE FURNITURE MATTE ☐ END TABLE (READY TO BE UPCYCLED) ☐ PAINT (CHOICE OF COLOR) ☐ PAINTBRUSH ☐ FRENCH GRAPHICS (ENLARGED TO FIT TABLE TOP) ☐ SANDER ☐ 80-GRIT SANDPAPER ☐ DRAWER HARDWARE, IF NEEDED ☐ SCREWDRIVER (TO ATTACH HARDWARE) ☐ RULER

WHAT YOU'LL DO

1 Remove drawer hardware using screwdriver.

2 Paint end table color of choice. Allow to dry.

3 When dry, distress piece with sander and 80-grit sandpaper to achieve vintage look.

4 Measure top of table. Add 2 inches (5 cm) to each side when enlarging French graphic print. Cut paper this size.

5 Using Mod Podge Furniture Matte, adhere paper to top of table. Make sure to center the design and allow paper to hang over on all four sides. Allow to dry.

6 When Mod Podged paper is completely dry, sand edges of table to remove the extra paper. This is an easy way to have the paper fit perfectly without stressing over exact measurements. The edges look wonderful when distressed (A).

7 Apply two to three topcoats of Mod Podge Furniture Matte to the tabletop, allowing each application to thoroughly dry before brushing on the next. Allow to dry.

8 Add hardware, if needed, to complete the updated look (B).

TROMPE L'OEIL DESK

DESIGNER: **Design Samaritan (Paul Bowman)**

Personalize a desk by creating an optical illusion using Mod Podge Photo Transfer Medium. By transferring photographs of actual objects, you can create a convincing illusion. Include personally significant objects to make the project unique and preserve them for years to come.

WHAT YOU'LL NEED MOD PODGE BASIC TOOL KIT (PAGE 18) ■ MOD PODGE FURNITURE MATTE ■ MOD PODGE PHOTO TRANSFER MEDIUM ■ DESK ■ WOOD STAIN ■ RAGS OR COTTON CLOTH ■ SPONGE ■ FOAM BRUSH ■ CAMERA ■ COLOR LASER COPIER

WHAT YOU'LL DO

1 Sand the top of the desk to remove any existing stain or varnish and to expose the wood.

2 Stain the top of the desk the color desired.

3 Select your objects to be photographed. Place each on the desk, in natural light for best results, and take a photo of each from above.

4 Print each photo on a color laser printer. Do not use an ink-jet printer. If the objects have any words, make sure to reverse the image when printing. This can either be done on the computer with photo editing software, or on a color laser copier. The image must be reversed so that once it is applied to the desktop, the words will be legible, as the image will be applied facedown.

5 Carefully cut each item out of the laser-printed photo copies, making sure to stay as close to the edges of the objects in the photos as possible.

6 On your work surface, apply Mod Podge Photo Transfer Medium to the image side of the cutouts (A). Make sure to apply an even layer, enough so you can barely see the image beneath the Mod Podge Photo Transfer Medium.

7 Invert the cutout and place on the desk in the desired position (B). Don't touch the area painted with the Mod Podge Photo Transfer Medium or fingerprints will transfer into the finished piece. Smooth out any bubbles from the center outward. Make sure there is full contact with the surface. If any excess Mod Podge Photo Transfer Medium is on the desk surface, wipe it up immediately with a damp cloth.

8 Let the photo transfers dry for 24 hours. Once dry, use a moistened sponge with clean water to soak the exposed paper. As the paper absorbs the water, it will become translucent and the image will appear. Let this sit for at least two minutes.

9 Using the damp sponge, rub in small circular motions until the paper starts to disintegrate (C). Rinse the sponge and carefully repeat this process until all the paper has been rubbed away. Don't rub too hard, or the image will be lost.

10 For added realism, create shadows under the photo-transferred objects by applying a slightly darker wood stain, using a paintbrush. Refer to the original photos for guidance on where the shadows fall to create the most realistic effect.

11 Cover the entire desktop surface with Mod Podge Furniture Matte. Let each coat dry for an hour before applying the next. A minimum of two coats is suggested. Let dry completely before use.

POSTER ART FURNITURE

DESIGNER: **Sherrie Ragsdale**

Take an old dresser and make it new again with some Mod Podge, some paint, and poster art.

WHAT YOU'LL NEED   MOD PODGE BASIC TOOL KIT (PAGE 18)   ☐   MOD PODGE FURNITURE SATIN   ☐
FOLKART MULTI-SURFACE PAINT, CARDINAL RED   ☐   DRESSER (NEW OR RECYCLED)   ☐
STENCIL TAPE   ☐   LARGE POSTER, BIG ENOUGH TO COVER FRONT OF DRESSER   ☐   SCREWDRIVER

WHAT YOU'LL DO

1   Remove any hardware that would get in the way of painting or decoupaging. Basecoat dresser with FolkArt Multi-Surface Paint in Cardinal Red. Allow to dry and then sand the edges to distress.

2   Place poster onto the dresser front, centering it evenly from furniture edges. Tape across each corner to hold it in place so that the edges of the poster are free. Outline the poster area by taping directly on the dresser front. This will mark where the poster was placed and will act as a placement guide once it is removed.

3   Place a piece of stencil tape on the dresser front at the top and bottom of the poster, still making sure the poster is staying within the tape outline. Find the openings around the drawers and cut through the poster with the craft knife. After all the sections are cut, the placement of the poster pieces on the drawer fronts should be easy using the taped outlines. You can lightly number poster pieces on their backs, if necessary, to keep them in order.

4   Mod Podge each poster section to the front of the dresser using tape marks as a guide, and be careful not to Mod Podge the tape itself. Allow to dry.

5   Remove the tape around the poster sections, and then add a topcoat of Mod Podge Furniture Satin (A). When the Mod Podge is dry, replace dresser drawer hardware.

RETRO REVIVAL

A gallery of retro-inspired projects with modern appeal,
with 1960s and 1970s eye-catching colors, bold graphics,
and classic surfaces made into fashion and home decor.
A homage to Mod Podge's beginnings.

GLITTER OMBRÉ CLOTHESPIN MIRROR

We all love glitter, right? When gazing into this glittered clothespin mirror, you cannot help but smile. Mod Podge and glitter are definitely a winning combo!

TOOLS AND MATERIALS MOD PODGE GLOSS ☐ ABOUT 45 WOOD CLOTHESPINS, OR AS MANY IT TAKES TO GO AROUND THE MIRROR ☐ ROUND MIRROR, AT LEAST 9 INCHES (22.9 CM) DIAMETER ☐ SPRAY PAINT, COORDINATING SHADE TO MATCH GLITTER COLORS ☐ 3 SHADES OF GLITTER ☐ TRAY (FOR CATCHING GLITTER) ☐ PAINTBRUSH ☐ MOD PODGE WONDER GLUE

WHAT YOU'LL DO

1 Begin by laying the clothespins out onto a large piece of paper; then spray-paint them. Be sure to do this outdoors or in a well-ventilated work space. Rotate the clothespins several times during this process, making sure all areas are painted. Let dry between coats.

2 Divide the clothespins into three equal piles for glittering.

3 One by one, add Mod Podge Gloss to the top of the clothespin with a paintbrush (A), and while the Mod Podge Gloss is still wet, sprinkle glitter directly on top (B). Tap the loose glitter off; then set clothespin aside to dry.

TIP: *Use a glitter tray to catch loose glitter so it can be reused.*

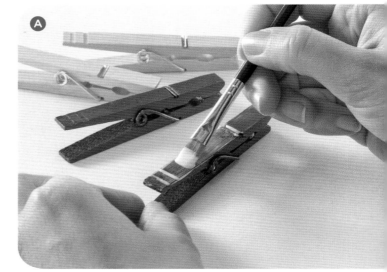

4 Repeat with all of the clothespins. The project shows three different glitter colors, approximately 15 clothespins for each glitter color, for a total of 45.

5 Once all clothespins are dry, brush excess glitter off into a trash bin, using a dry paintbrush.

6 Place clothespins around the outside of the mirror; do this at first with no glue to check for equal spacing.

7 When the clothespins are evenly spaced around the mirror, begin to glue each clothespin down (one by one), with Mod Podge Wonder Glue, until all are secured.

8 Let dry for 24 hours before hanging.

CANDY WRAPPER SHADOW BOXES

Candy wrappers are usually filled with bright colors and fun patterns, making them the perfect material for collage. For this project. we designed three unique looks, all using candy wrappers from our local Japanese dollar store. If you want to keep the wrappers for future projects, we suggest color copying them instead of using originals.

WHAT YOU'LL NEED MOD PODGE BASIC TOOL KIT (PAGE 18) ■ MOD PODGE GLOSS ■ MOD PODGE CRAFT MAT ■ 3 SHADOW BOX FRAMES ■ CANDY WRAPPERS (ORIGINALS OR PHOTOCOPIES) ■ FOR STRAWBERRY SHADOW BOX: PINK PAPER, THE SIZE OF SHADOW BOX ■ FOR FLOWER SHADOW BOX: FLOWER PAPER PUNCH OR SCISSORS ■ FOR FLOWER SHADOW BOX: BLUE PAPER, THE SIZE OF SHADOW BOX ■ FOR FLOWER SHADOW BOX: FLAT-BACKED PEARLS AND GEMS ■ FOR FLOWER SHADOW BOX: MOD PODGE WONDER GLUE

WHAT YOU'LL DO

STRAWBERRY SHADOW BOX

1 Remove backing from frame. Cut the pink paper to fit the inside the frame.

2 Cut a large motif from a candy wrapper, or from an enlargement of one (A).

3 Apply Mod Podge Gloss to the back of the motif and glue to the center of the pink paper. Allow to dry.

4 Cut candy wrappers to fit around the outer edge of the frame. Apply Mod Podge Gloss to the back of the candy wrappers, position on the frame, and press with your fingers to remove any air bubbles. Then topcoat with more Mod Podge Gloss (B). Overlap the wrappers as needed. Allow to dry.

5 Return backing to the frame.

RAINBOW SHADOW BOX

1 Remove backing from the frame.

2 Gather candy wrappers by the seven colors of the rainbow.

3 Using a ruler, mark seven equal-sized vertical sections on the frame backing. The rightmost section will be red and the leftmost section will be purple.

4 Cut the candy wrappers into small strips or motifs, keeping them arranged by color.

5 Apply Mod Podge Gloss to the backs of the candy wrapper pieces, and position them on the frame backing in the proper

section, by color. Press with your fingers to remove any air bubbles, and topcoat with Mod Podge Gloss. Overlap the wrappers as needed. Allow to dry.

6 Return backing to the frame.

FLOWER SHADOW BOX

1 Remove backing from the frame. Cut the blue paper to fit inside the backing of the frame.

2 Gather candy wrappers by color, purples and blues.

3 Punch flowers from the wrappers, or cut flowers with scissors.

4 Apply Mod Podge Gloss to the backs of the flower-shaped cutouts. Beginning in one corner, apply the flowers in a cluster onto the blue paper. Press with your fingers to remove any air bubbles. Overlap the flower cutouts as needed. Add more flowers to the design, working toward the opposite corner. Allow to dry.

5 Attach gems and pearls randomly to the centers of the flowers with Mod Podge Wonder Glue. Allow to dry.

6 Return backing to the frame.

TV TRAY
MAKEOVER

DESIGNER: **David Cheaney**

TV TRAY MAKEOVER

TV trays are incredibly useful (not just for meals) and can be found in almost any thrift store. Even if they are beat up and grubby, some quick work with paint, paper, and Mod Podge can make them a stylish addition to any home.

WHAT YOU'LL NEED MOD PODGE BASIC TOOL KIT (PAGE 18) ■ MOD PODGE FURNITURE SATIN ■ TV TRAY ■ SPRAY PAINT (COLOR TO COORDINATE WITH PAPER) ■ PAPER (FOR TEMPLATE), 8½ x 11 INCHES (21.6 x 27.9 CM) ■ DECORATIVE PAPER FOR TRAY ■ 400-GRIT WET-DRY SANDPAPER ■ CELLOPHANE TAPE

WHAT YOU'LL DO

1 Tape together several pieces of paper larger than the center of the tray. Use this paper to create a template or pattern the shape of the interior of tray. Turn the tray upside down, and trace around the shape of the bottom of the tray on the paper (A).

2 Give the tray two or three light coats of spray paint. Be sure to do this outdoors or in a well-ventilated place.

3 Cut out the template (B). Flip TV tray over and place cut pattern on tray interior to check for correct sizing (C).

4 Trace the template shape onto the back of the decorative paper, using a pencil. Cut out decorative paper along the pencil lines.

5 Spread Mod Podge Furniture Satin on the tray interior and on the back of the decorative paper. Lay the paper on the tray and gently smooth it out, using damp fingertips or a foam brush. Work from the center outward. Take up any excess Mod Podge with a cloth.

6 When the paper has dried thoroughly, topcoat with several layers of Mod Podge Furniture Satin, wet sanding gently between coats (using 400-grit sandpaper is desirable), to create an extra-smooth finish.

GRAPHIC POSTER FILE CABINET

DESIGNER: ***Julie Lewis***

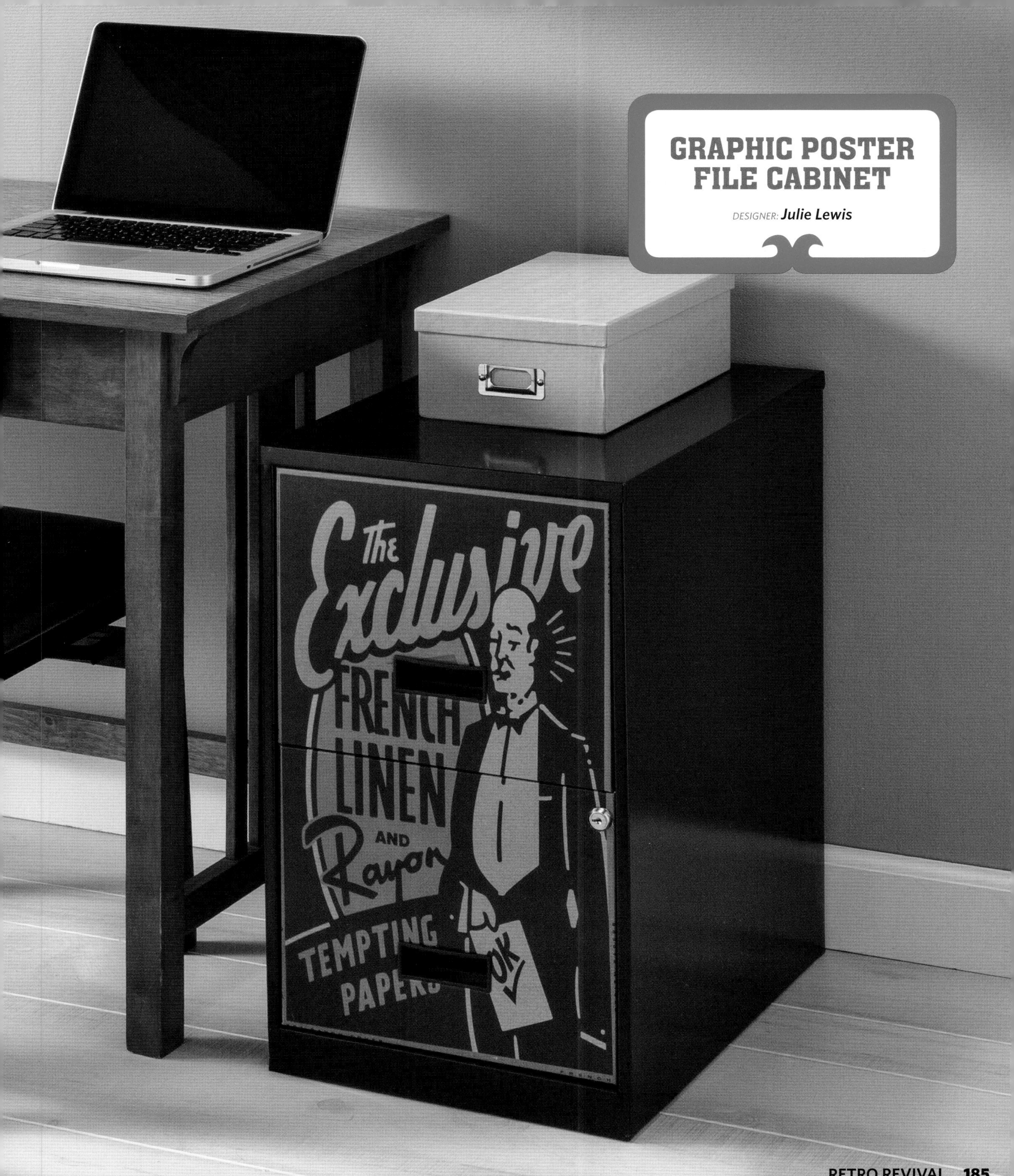

GRAPHIC POSTER FILE CABINET

A plain file cabinet is transformed into something upscale with the application of an eye-catching poster.

WHAT YOU'LL NEED   MOD PODGE BASIC TOOL KIT (PAGE 18) ■ MOD PODGE FURNITURE GLOSS ■ TWO-DRAWER METAL FILE CABINET ■ PHOTOCOPY OF POSTER ■ TOOLS NEEDED TO REMOVE HARDWARE FROM CABINET FRONT

WHAT YOU'LL DO

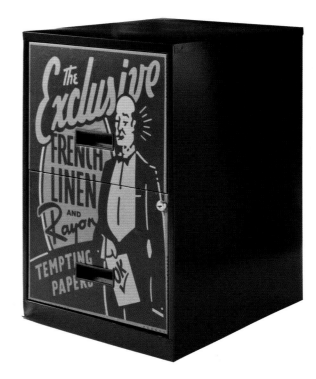

1 Resize and photocopy the poster image to fit filing cabinet drawer fronts. Cut photocopy in half horizontally to fit upper and lower drawers.

2 Remove all hardware from the front of cabinet, if possible.

3 Brush Mod Podge Furniture Gloss onto a drawer front and apply photocopy. Smooth as much as possible with fingers; then cover with waxed paper. Use Mod Podge Squeegee to smooth out any remaining bubbles. Repeat process with second drawer. Carefully cut out paper around any raised or depressed areas (such as the lock or finger grips) with a craft knife (A).

4 Let Mod Podge Furniture Gloss dry for 20 minutes; then apply additional coats to seal. Upon application, paper may bubble, but it will flatten out as the Mod Podge dries.

5 Replace all hardware before using cabinet.

FOUND OBJECT DECORATIVE BUST

DESIGNER: *Julie Lewis*

FOUND OBJECT DECORATIVE BUST

Experience the creative satisfaction of taking an everyday found object and transforming it into something totally different with just paint, rice paper, and Mod Podge.

WHAT YOU'LL NEED MOD PODGE BASIC TOOL KIT (PAGE 18) ▪ MOD PODGE MATTE ▪ FOLKART MULTI-SURFACE PAINT, PEARL BLUE TAFFETA ▪ DECORATIVE FOUND OBJECT, PLASTER BUST ▪ CROSSHATCH RICE PAPER ▪ SCISSORS ▪ ¾-INCH (19 MM) FLAT BRUSH

WHAT YOU'LL DO

1 Basecoat the bust with FolkArt Multi-Surface Paint in Pearl Blue Taffeta. Apply several coats, allowing drying time between applications.

2 Cut rice paper into small and large squares, approximately ½ inch (1.3 cm) and 1 inch (2.5 cm) size.

3 Brush Mod Podge Matte onto painted bust surface; apply a rice paper square. Smooth with brush (A) and continue applying additional squares. overlapping slightly. Cut smaller pieces where needed to fit into small recessed areas or curved areas on bust. Continue until the entire bust is covered. Let dry at least 20 minutes.

4 Seal decoupaged bust with several coats of Mod Podge Matte, allowing dry time between applications.

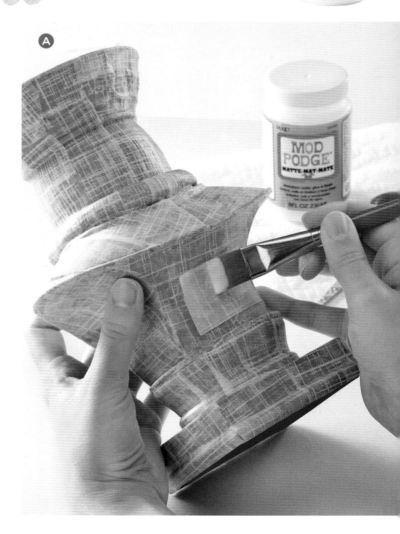

Ⓐ

STARBURST PAINT STIR STICK WALL CLOCK

DESIGNER: ***Julie Lewis***

STARBURST PAINT STIR STICK WALL CLOCK

Inspired by the sleek lines and retro graphics of the mid-century Modern era, this Starburst Clock will pump up the level of coolness in any room.

WHAT YOU'LL NEED MOD PODGE BASIC TOOL KIT (PAGE 18) ☐ MOD PODGE GLOSS ☐ FOLKART ACRYLIC PAINT, SILVER STERLING ☐ 22 WOOD PAINT STIR STICKS ☐ JIGSAW ☐ ASSORTED RETRO-PATTERNED SCRAPBOOK PAPERS ☐ PHOTOCOPY OF A CLOCK FACE (SIZED TO FIT ROUND PLAQUE) ☐ 6 ½-INCH DIAMETER (16.5 CM) ROUND WOOD PLAQUE ☐ HAND DRILL AND DRILL BIT ☐ CLOCK MECHANISM ☐ WAXED PAPER ☐ HOT GLUE GUN AND GLUE STICKS

WHAT YOU'LL DO

1 Cut 11 of the 22 wood paint stir sticks to measure 9 inches (22.9 cm) long. Trace all paint stir sticks, cut and uncut, onto a scrapbook paper and cut out paper (A). Vary choices of paper to give good variety of colors and patterns. Also cut out the clock face photocopy, which has been sized fit round plaque.

2 Paint the round plaque using FolkArt Acrylic Paint in Silver Sterling. When dry, find the center of the plaque and drill a hole through the plaque large enough for the shaft of clock mechanism to fit.

3 Brush Mod Podge Gloss onto a paint stir stick and apply cut paper. Cover with waxed paper and smooth out bubbles with Mod Podge Squeegee. Repeat for the remaining 21 paint stir sticks. Brush surface of plaque with Mod Podge Gloss and repeat process for clock face. Let all paper dry for 20 minutes before applying additional coats of Mod Podge Gloss to seal (B). Carefully use craft knife to cut open the circle in center of clock face for the shaft of the clockworks.

4 Turn circle plaque over. Starting with the shortened stir sticks, hot-glue around the back edge of plaque, spacing equally. Repeat with larger sticks, gluing them on top of and between smaller sticks. Let dry.

5 Following clock mechanism instructions that came with clock parts purchase, attach the mechanism and hands to clock.

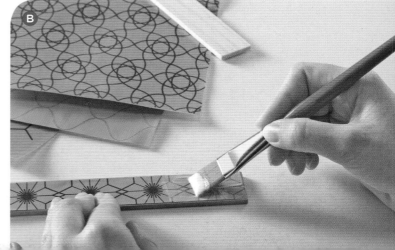

ARTFUL TREE CANVAS

DESIGNER: **Julie Lewis**

ARTFUL TREE CANVAS

An oversized canvas displays a tree adorned with brightly colored leaves to make a bold and colorful statement.

WHAT YOU'LL NEED MOD PODGE BASIC TOOL KIT (PAGE 18) ☐ MOD PODGE GLOSS ☐ MOD PODGE SHEER COLORS: BROWN, AQUA, ORANGE, RED, GREEN, YELLOW, AND PURPLE ☐ FOLKART ACRYLIC PAINT, WICKER WHITE ☐ SIMPLY STENCILS CUT-YOUR-OWN-STENCIL BLANKS ☐ PALETTE KNIFE ☐ TISSUE PAPER SHEETS FROM OLD SEWING PATTERNS ☐ 24 x 24-INCH (61 x 61 CM) STRETCHED CANVAS ☐ TRANSFER PAPER ☐ ROUND BRUSH ☐ TEMPLATES (PAGE 229)

WHAT YOU'LL DO

1 Using a palette knife, spread a layer of Mod Podge Sheer Colors onto a stencil blank. Repeat on other stencil blanks to make layers of a variety of colors. Set aside to dry overnight.

2 Tear dress pattern tissue paper into various shapes and sizes. Starting anywhere on the canvas, brush Mod Podge Gloss onto the canvas surface; apply torn pattern tissue. Then brush the tissue with Mod Podge Gloss while pressing paper in place to adhere. Continue covering surface of canvas, slightly overlapping pieces of tissue to create extra depth of color. Let dry 20 minutes before sealing entire canvas with another coat of Mod Podge Gloss.

3 Trace tree pattern found in the Template section. Cut the pattern, then trace onto canvas. Paint tree with FolkArt Acrylic Paint in Wicker White using a round paintbrush. Allow to dry. Reapply a second coat of Wicker White, if necessary.

4 Cut leaves from dried Mod Podge Sheer Color by placing leaf pattern under the stencil blank and cutting out leaves with craft knife. Then lift tip of leaf with knife; pull from stencil blank (A) and place leaf near tree limb. Continue placing leaves around tree limbs (B). Mod Podge Sheer Color leaves will cling to the canvas. Refer to photo for color and placement.

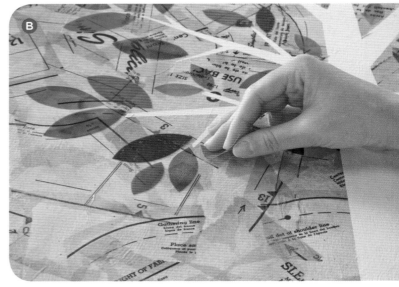

LINOLEUM FLOORCLOTH

DESIGNER: *Julie Lewis*

LINOLEUM FLOORCLOTH

Enrich your everyday life experience with something as simple as a unique floorcloth, personally designed by you.

WHAT YOU'LL NEED MOD PODGE BASIC TOOL KIT (PAGE 18) ■ MOD PODGE FURNITURE GLOSS ■ FOLKART MULTI-SURFACE PAINT: YELLOW OCHRE AND PURE ORANGE ■ 24 x 36-INCH (61 x 91 CM) OR LARGER LINOLEUM REMNANT ■ PAINTER'S TAPE ■ SIX 10-INCH-SQUARE (25.4 CM) PIECES OF SCRAPBOOK PAPER ■ MOD PODGE 4-INCH (10.2 CM) BRUSH APPLICATOR

WHAT YOU'LL DO

1 Measure and cut linoleum 24 x 36 inches (61 x 91 cm). Turn over to use the back of linoleum as the crafting surface.

2 Measure and tape off a 2-inch (5 cm) border. Using FolkArt Multi-Surface Paint, paint border Yellow Ochre. Let dry. Carefully remove tape.

3 Measure and tape off 1-inch (2.5 cm) border inside the Yellow Ochre border. Using FolkArt Multi-Surface Paint, paint interior border Pure Orange. Let dry. Carefully remove tape.

4 Lay the scrapbook paper squares out so they cover the entire floorcloth. Starting in the center of one long side of the floorcloth, brush Mod Podge Furniture Gloss onto the linoleum under the center square; then apply a 10-inch (25.4 cm) scrapbook paper square. Cover with waxed paper and smooth with Mod Podge Squeegee. Repeat process adding paper squares to either side of the first decoupaged square.

5 Apply remaining squares along opposite edge of floorcloth until entire center area of linoleum is covered to the borders. Let floorcloth dry 20 minutes after you apply last piece of paper.

6 Seal the entire floorcloth with additional coats of Mod Podge Furniture (A). The linoleum may buckle or warp initially (B) but will relax over time. Allow to dry thoroughly before use.

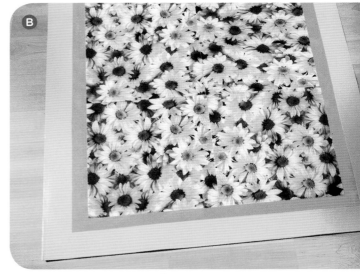

DESIGNER: **Design Samaritan (Paul Bowman)**

DRESSER DRAWER WALL VALET

DRESSER DRAWER WALL VALET

What do you do with a lone dresser drawer? Create a valet to hold cosmetics, perfume, jewelry, scarves, and other accessories . . . that's what I do!

WHAT YOU'LL NEED MOD PODGE BASIC TOOL KIT (PAGE 18) ▫ MOD PODGE FURNITURE MATTE ▫ SCREWDRIVER ▫ DRILL AND DRILL BIT TO MAKE HOLES FOR DOWELS ▫ DRESSER DRAWER ▫ STAINABLE WOOD PUTTY ▫ WOOD STAIN TO MATCH DRAWER ▫ PAINT FOR DRAWER (IF YOU WANT TO CHANGE ITS COLOR) ▫ DECORATIVE PAPER (WALLPAPER, WRAPPING PAPER, SCRAPBOOKING PAPER, ETC.) FOR INTERIOR OF DRAWER ▫ TWO ⅜-INCH (9.5 MM) WOODEN DOWELS, AS LONG AS THE WIDTH OF THE DRAWER PLUS AN INCH (2.5 CM) ▫ WOOD GLUE (OPTIONAL) ▫ TWO PICTURE FRAME HANGERS (CORRECT SIZE FOR WEIGHT OF DRAWER) ▫ PICTURE FRAME WIRE ▫ MIRROR (CUT TO FIT THE DRAWER INTERIOR; ORDER A CUSTOM SIZE FROM A PROFESSIONAL GLASS VENDOR) ▫ MIRROR ADHESIVE ▫ PUTTY KNIFE

WHAT YOU'LL DO

1 Remove any hardware from drawer (pulls, etc.).

2 Fill the holes that remain after removing the hardware with wood putty. Use a stainable putty, or one that matches the finish of the drawer.

3 Sand and reapply wood putty until all holes are filled and flush with drawer surface. Add any stain required to the putty, to match the color of the drawer. If painting the drawer, do that before step 4.

4 Cut decorative paper to fit the interior sides of the drawer. Pay special attention to the pattern repeat, and align the pattern at the corners.

5 Apply decorative paper using Mod Podge Furniture Matte. First, apply Mod Podge Furniture Matte to the inner surface of the drawer side or front, and then apply Mod Podge Furniture Matte to the back of the paper to be applied. Gently lay the paper on the drawer interior; smooth out bubbles, working from the center of the paper to the edges.

6 Once dry, apply a thin coat of Mod Podge Furniture Matte on top of the paper, making sure to seal the edges (A). Let dry at least one hour and repeat.

7 On two sides of the drawer, locate holes for the dowels by measuring and marking with a pencil. Drill four ⅜-inch

Ⓐ

(9.5 mm) holes, two for each dowel. Insert the wood dowels into the holes. Add wood glue to secure the dowels at each end before inserting if desired. Dowel rods become organizational storage for necklaces, scarves, etc.

8 Add two picture frame hangers on the back of the drawer (one on each side) by predrilling holes to fit the wood screws supplied with the appropriate hanger. Attach picture frame wire to span between the hangers.

9 Using mirror adhesive, apply a liberal amount to the back of the mirror and place the mirror inside the drawer where desired. Follow directions on adhesive for drying time.

AQUA BLUE GLASS LAMP

Adding sheer color to a clear glass lamp will add a pop of color to any nightstand or end table.

WHAT YOU'LL NEED ☐ MOD PODGE GLOSS ☐ MOD PODGE SHEER COLOR, AQUA ☐ CLEAR GLASS LAMP (WITH HOLE IN BOTTOM) ☐ MEASURING CUP ☐ MIXING CUP ☐ FORK ☐ STENCIL TAPE ☐ WAX PAPER

WHAT YOU'LL DO

1 In a mixing cup, pour 1 cup (240 mL) Mod Podge Gloss. Then add 1 cup (240 mL) Mod Podge Sheer Color Aqua (A).

2 Using a fork, gently mix until thoroughly blended (B).

3 Remove the lamp's electrical cord and fittings so they do not interfere with the lamp and with the Mod Podge mixture.

4 Pour the paint mixture into the bottom of the lamp and swirl it around until the entire inside of the glass lamp is covered (C).

5 Elevate the lamp so excess paint mixture may drip from the open lamp base onto the waxed paper. Allow to dry completely before reassembling.

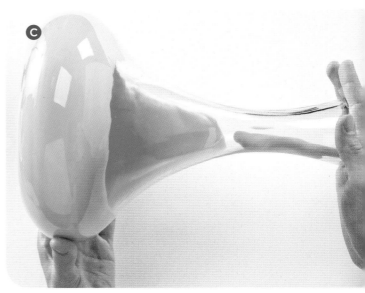

B

A

C

HANDMADE CREATIONS FOR HOLIDAYS AND CELEBRATIONS

Here are some festive ideas for holiday decorating, gift giving, and special occasions throughout the year.

THE BIG BOOK OF MOD PODGE®

VALENTINE TREAT JARS

DESIGNER: *Candie Cooper*

Romance is in the air on Valentine's Day, so make these deliciously romantic glass jars to hold some fancy chocolates for that special someone.

WHAT YOU'LL NEED MOD PODGE BASIC TOOL KIT (PAGE 18) ▢ MOD PODGE ANTIQUE MATTE ▢ MOD PODGE MOD MELTER ▢ MOD PODGE MOD MELT, SEA GLASS CLEAR ▢ MOD PODGE MOD MOLD, FLOWERS ▢ FOLKART ACRYLIC PAINT, PURE GOLD ▢ COLOR PHOTOCOPY OF VINTAGE VALENTINE IMAGE FOR JAR ▢ GLASS JAR (WITH LID) ▢ HIGH TEMPERATURE GLUE GUN ▢ SMALL FLAT-BACK CRYSTAL ▢ SPOOL OF DECORATIVE TRIM ▢ GREEN VELVET LEAVES

WHAT YOU'LL DO

1 Cut out the vintage valentine image with scissors.

2 Paint a coat of Mod Podge Antique Matte on top of the image, and set it aside on a nonstick surface to dry.

3 Insert the Mod Podge Sea Glass Mod Melt into the Mod Podge Mod Melter and fill the rose-shaped Mod Podge Mod Mold following the manufacturer's instructions. Let rose embellishment cool completely before removing.

4 Paint a layer of Mod Podge Antique Matte onto the back of your image and place on the jar (A). Smooth out with fingers, taking care that Mod Podge doesn't ooze out from edges. If it does, wipe away with lightly dampened paper towel. Allow to dry.

5 Hot-glue the trim in place around the base of the jar and around the knob of the lid.

6 Using FolkArt Acrylic Paint, color the Mod Podge Mod Melt rose embellishment Pure Gold. Allow to dry. If desired, place a dot of Mod Podge Antique Matte in the center; adhere crystal in the center of the flower.

7 Hot-glue velvet leaves and flower to the top of the jar (B). Fill jar with treats!

VALENTINE'S DAY BOX

DESIGNER: **Chris Williams**

Valentine's Day is a special day for little ones at school, especially when it is time to share their valentines with classmates and friends. Create a special Valentine's Day container with your little ones this year. They will love you for it!

WHAT YOU'LL NEED MOD PODGE BASIC TOOL KIT (PAGE 18) ▪ MOD PODGE MATTE ▪ FOLKART MULTI-SURFACE PAINTS: MAGENTA AND BURNT UMBER ▪ MOD PODGE MOD MELTER ▪ MOD PODGE MELTS, SEA GLASS CLEAR ▪ CEREAL BOX ▪ ASSORTED SCRAPBOOK PAPERS FOR MONKEY AND HEART ▪ WHITE POSTER BOARD ▪ NO. 1 LINER BRUSH ▪ MAGENTA ORGANZA RIBBON ▪ TRACING PAPER ▪ MONKEY TEMPLATES (PAGE 232)

WHAT YOU'LL DO

1 Prepare the empty cereal box by removing the interior cellophane bag. Using a craft knife and the larger heart pattern from the Template section, carefully cut a large heart-shaped opening into the front of the box (A). This will be the opening in which the Valentine will be placed.

2 With FolkArt Multi-Surface Acrylic Paint, color the interior of the box Magenta (B), and paint the exterior of the box Burnt Umber. Allow to dry and reapply a second coat of paint to each section.

3 While the paint is drying, begin cutting monkey paper shapes (eyes, nose, cheeks, face, arms, belly, tail and heart), using the patterns found in the Template section of the book. Patterns can be cut from a variety of monkey-colored and monkey-patterned papers; be creative!

TIP: *Creating the patterns is easy; they can be photocopied or can be created using artist's tracing paper and a marker.*

4 Once the patterns are created and papers cut, the fun of Mod Podging them to create the monkey begins. To give a little more stability to the head, tail, and largest heart, decoupage the patterned papers to white poster board. Apply Mod Podge Matte to the back of the paper and to the poster board surface. Smooth in place (C).

5 Place a piece of waxed paper over the surface and press a Mod Podge Squeegee over the waxed paper to remove excess Mod Podge and to firmly adhere the paper to the poster board, working from the center outward (D). Allow to dry for 10 minutes. Next, apply a coat of Mod Podge Matte over the top of the decoupaged paper, extending a bit onto the white poster board. Allow to dry.

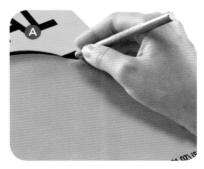

VALENTINE'S DAY BOX

6 Continue "building" the monkey's face by adding additional layers of paper; (face, eyes, nose, and cheeks). Brush a final coat of Mod Podge Matte over the monkey's head and allow to dry.

7 Cut the tail, heart, and monkey head from the white poster board. Be sure to cut close to the printed paper, so that you do not have a white poster board halo on the edges.

8 With FolkArt Multi-Surface Paint. color the back surface of the monkey's tail, arms, and head Burnt Umber, and paint the back surface of the heart Magenta. Allow to dry, and reapply paint until opaque.

9 Next, decoupage the monkey tummy directly onto the box front, centering over the cut heart opening. In the heart area, fold excess paper inward and adhere to the box interior using Mod Podge Matte.

10 Using a No. 1 liner brush and FolkArt Multi-Surface Paint in Magenta, paint a smile on the monkey face, connecting the two heart cheeks.

11 Still working with the No. 1 liner brush and FolkArt Multi-Surface Paint, apply Burnt Umber to "Be Mine," a running-stitch line, and small hearts on the larger heart shape.

12 Hot-glue the monkey tail to the back of the box bottom. Attach the arms to the front of the box on either side of the heart opening. Attach the head just above the heart opening, on top of the arms. Last, attach the "Be Mine" heart to one monkey paw.

13 If desired, cut additional cheek- and nose-sized hearts and Mod Podge them to the sides of the box.

14 Tie magenta organza ribbon into a bow and hot-glue it to the monkey's chin using Mod Podge Sea Glass Clear Mod Melts and the Mod Podge Mod Melter.

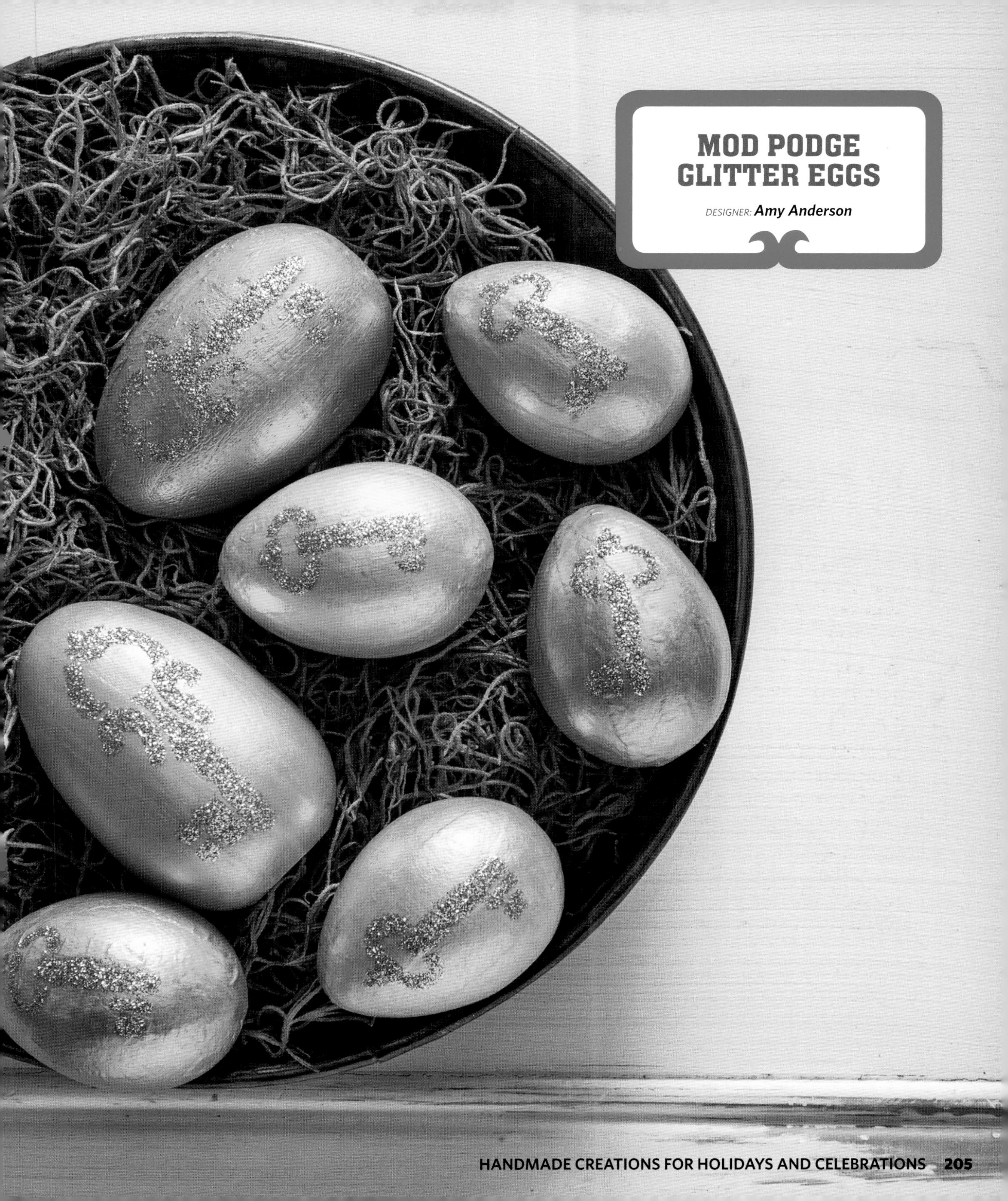

MOD PODGE GLITTER EGGS

DESIGNER: ***Amy Anderson***

MOD PODGE GLITTER EGGS

Decorating with stylish eggs is so fun any time of the year; in spring, adding pizzazz with metallic colors and sparkly glitter makes it even more fun.

WHAT YOU'LL NEED   MOD PODGE GLOSS   ☐   MOD PODGE ROCKS! PEEL & STICK STENCILS: SKELETON KEYS   ☐   MOD PODGE SPOUNCERS   ☐   FOLKART ACRYLIC PAINTS, COPPER AND PURE GOLD   ☐   PAPIER-MÂCHÉ OR WOOD EGGS   ☐   MOD PODGE PODGEABLE GLITTER   ☐   SOFT BRISTLE PAINTBRUSH

WHAT YOU'LL DO

1 Paint the eggs with several coats of metallic paint, creating opaque coverage. Allow to dry thoroughly between coats.

2 Remove the Mod Podge Rocks! Peel & Stick Skeleton Key Stencil from the backer sheet and place onto an egg, centering the design. Smooth with fingers.

3 Use a Mod Podge Spouncer to apply Mod Podge Gloss to the stencil design (A). Remove the stencil immediately.

4 Sprinkle glitter on top of the design and let dry (B). If desired, use a contrasting glitter color for a "pop" of color. While your glitter design is drying, wash the stencil and return to the backer sheet.

5 When the glitter and Mod Podge are dry, use a soft bristle paintbrush to brush away excess glitter.

6 Repeat stencil and glitter process with remaining eggs.

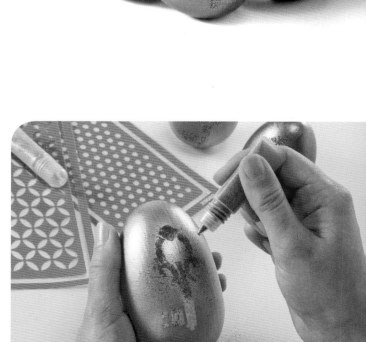

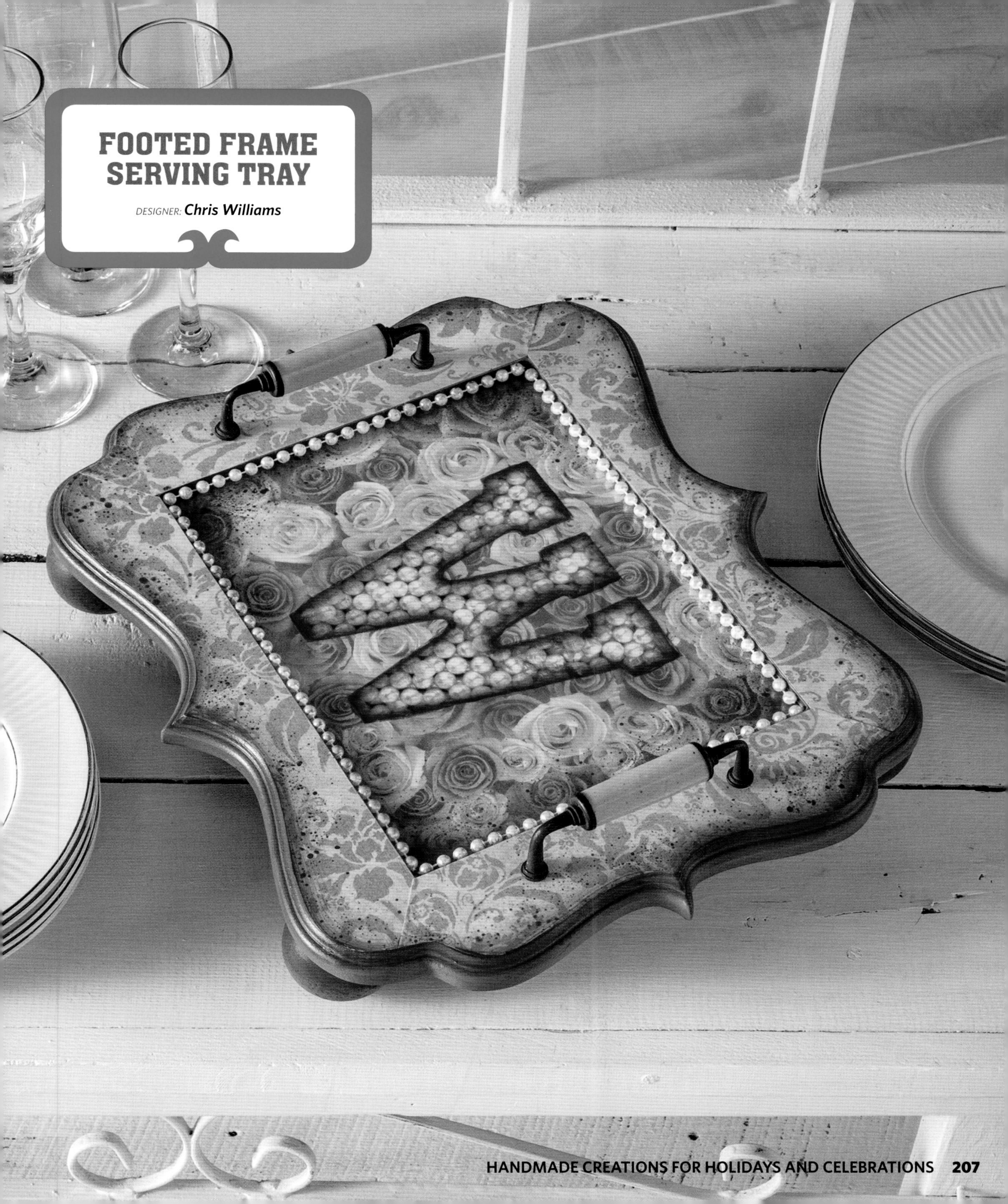

FOOTED FRAME SERVING TRAY

DESIGNER: ***Chris Williams***

FOOTED FRAME SERVING TRAY

Enjoying an elegant serving tray with a vintage, romantic feel would be awesome for a wedding or for the Christmas holidays. You too, can create one by upcycling a frame, using Mod Podge and by adding feet and handles!

WHAT YOU'LL NEED   MOD PODGE BASIC TOOL KIT (PAGE 18) ■ MOD PODGE MATTE ■ FOLKART MULTI-SURFACE PAINTS: COFFEE LATTE AND BARK BROWN ■ WOOD PICTURE FRAME WITH GLASS AND WOOD BACKING ■ FOUR 2-INCH (5CM) WOOD BALL KNOBS ■ 2 DECORATIVE METAL HANDLES AND SCREWS TO HOLD THEM ■ 3 ASSORTED SCRAPBOOK PAPERS, WITH COORDINATING PATTERNS AND COLORS ■ OLD TOOTHBRUSH ■ RUBBING ALCOHOL ■ MOD PODGE WONDER GLUE ■ HAND OR ELECTRIC DRILL AND DRILL BIT TO FIT SCREW SIZE ■ STRING OF PLASTIC WHITE PEARLS (LENGTH OF FRAME OPENING CIRCUMFERENCE) ■ SCREWDRIVER

WHAT YOU'LL DO

1 Begin by removing the glass and the wood backing and mounting board (if any) from the frame and set aside.

2 Cut scrapbook paper to match frame shape and size. If the frame is too large to fit on one paper, cut one paper pattern to fit each side of the frame and miter the corners of the paper. Set papers aside for now.

3 Paint the routed edges of the frame as well as the inside edge Bark Brown and allow to dry.

4 Determine placement of handles on two sides of the frame and mark with a pencil. Drill holes for screws of handle.

5 Measure, mark, and cut a full sheet of paper to fit the frame's mounting board or backing. Cut a letter from a coordinating paper to personalize with a family initial.

TIP: *Letters can be cut by tracing around pre-made wood or chipboard letters, by tracing inside a stencil, or by printing a favorite typeface from the computer.*

6 With Mod Podge Matte, apply the paper you cut out in step 2 to frame. Also Mod Podge papers cut in step 5 to backing or to mounting board of frame and allow to dry. Apply paper letter to center of backing insert or mounting board using Mod Podge Matte. When dry, brush a coat of Mod Podge Matte over all the surfaces. Let dry.

7 To give the entire project an antiqued, vintage feel, load a ¾-inch (19 mm) flat brush with Mod Podge Matte; add FolkArt Multi-Surface Paint in Bark Brown to one side of the flat brush. Brush along the edge of the frame, along the backing edges, and along the cut paper letter edges, keeping the brown paint to the outside edge (A). Allow this to dry, and reapply if a more antiqued look is desired. Allow to dry.

8 Enhance the vintage feel with a little color splattering or flyspecking. Thin FolkArt Multi-Surface Paint in Bark Brown with a touch of water and tap an old toothbrush into the thinned paint. With the bristles facing downward, rake the bristles of the toothbrush over your finger, forcing tiny specks of color to fly out onto the surface (B). Allow to dry.

9 Apply FolkArt Multi-Surface Paint in Coffee Latte to the four wood ball knobs and antique, using the techniques described above. Antique the section of each knob that comes closest to the frame base.

10 Change the white pearl beads to vintage-like pearls by brushing a coat of FolkArt Multi-Surface Paint in Coffee Latte over the pearls.

TIP: *Do not paint each bead; just brush color over the whole string with a "hit or miss" technique. Allow to dry.*

11 Clean the glass by wiping with a paper towel moistened with rubbing alcohol. Assemble the frame by replacing the glass, mounting board (if there was one), and backing. Using Mod Podge Wonder Glue, glue the painted pearl beads to the inner frame edge, around the glass.

12 Screw the handles in place on the frame sides.

TIP: *To fully secure the handles, add a drop of Mod Podge Wonder Glue to the screw opening before screwing the handle in place.*

13 Glue the four painted wood knobs onto the base of the frame using Mod Podge Wonder Glue and allow to set before using.

FOURTH-OF-JULY TABLE AND SERVING SET

DESIGNER: **Sherrie Ragsdale**

The fireworks will be unimportant, compared to the large impression made with this fun and festive table set.

WHAT YOU'LL NEED   MOD PODGE BASIC TOOL KIT (PAGE 18)   ▢   MOD PODGE MATTE   ▢   MOD PODGE SHEER COLOR, BLUE   ▢   FOLKART ACRYLIC PAINTS: CARDINAL RED, COFFEE BEAN, AND CALYPSO SKY   ▢   FOLKART MULTI-SURFACE PAINT, PARCHMENT   ▢   OUTDOOR TABLE   ▢   RED, WHITE, AND BLUE SCRAPBOOK PAPERS (ASSORTED PATTERNS)   ▢   ½-INCH-THICK (1.3 CM) BIRCH PLYWOOD, 12 x 18 INCHES (30.5 CM x 45.7 CM)   ▢   FAUX WOOD GRAIN SCRAPBOOK PAPER   ▢   TWINE   ▢   EIGHT 2-INCH (5 CM) WOOD STARS   ▢   THIN NAILS, FOR ATTACHING WOOD STARS   ▢   HAMMER   ▢   CLEAR GLASS DINNER PLATES   ▢   CLEAR GLASS JAR   ▢   1-INCH (2.5 CM) WOOD STAR   ▢   STENCIL BRUSH   ▢   MOD PODGE WONDER GLUE

WHAT YOU'LL DO:

TABLE

1   Create a flag design on the tabletop, by cutting different patterned paper strips of red, white, and blue scrapbook paper. With Mod Podge Matte, apply paper strips to the table to form the American flag, or whatever design you like. Let dry.

2   When dry, brush additional coats of Mod Podge Matte allowing each coat to dry thoroughly before applying the next.

TRAY

1   To create the tray, apply FolkArt Acrylic Paint in Cardinal Red to the plywood, and allow to dry.

2   Mod Podge faux wood grain scrapbook paper onto the tray. Allow to dry.

3   Using a stencil brush, paint FolkArt Acrylic Paint in Cardinal Red around the edges of the paper on top of the tray, fading it as you go toward the center (A). Allow to dry.

4   Using FolkArt Acrylic Paint in Coffee Bean, drybrush around the edges to age.

5   Cut six white-and-blue scrapbook paper stars out and Mod Podge them flat into the corners of the tray, with parts of the stars falling off the corners. Overlap as you go.

6   Cut four pieces of twine 10 inches (25.4 cm) long and glue into swirls on two opposite corners of the tray, two on each corner (see photo). Allow to dry.

7   Using FolkArt Acrylic Paint, paint eight 2-inch wood stars Calypso Sky, let dry, and then drybrush with Coffee Bean. Glue into place on the sides of the corners, for the legs of the tray. Secure each with a couple of nails.

FOURTH-OF-JULY TABLE AND SERVING SET

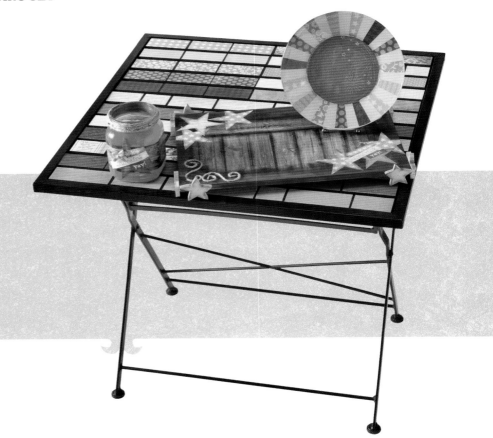

PLATES

1 For each plate, cut out a circle from the red scrapbook paper and Mod Podge onto the back of the glass plate, with the pattern facing toward the front.

2 Cut strips of different patterns of blue scrapbook paper and Mod Podge around the red circle, also on the back of the plate, with patterns facing toward the front. Allow to dry.

3 With FolkArt Multi-Surface Paint, paint the back of the plate in Parchment. Allow to thoroughly dry before using.

NOTE: *This plate should be created for decorative purposes only. It is not dishwasher safe.*

JAR

1 Pour Mod Podge Sheer Color Blue inside the jar; swirl to coat interior of jar; turn jar upside down and allow excess to drain. Allow to dry upside down overnight.

2 Cut a 2½-inch (6.4 cm) strip of the faux wood scrapbook paper, and apply as a center band to outside of the jar with Mod Podge Matte.

3 Apply a red paper star with Mod Podge and add some text from the scrapbook papers over it.

4 Paint the 1-inch (2.5 cm) small wood star with FolkArt Multi-Surface Paint in Calypso Sky; let dry. Tie a piece of twine in a knot and glue onto the front of the star. Glue the star to the front of the jar using Mod Podge Wonder Glue. Wrap twine around the top of the jar.

NOTE: *This jar is for decorative use only; it is not dishwasher safe.*

FALL CENTERPIECE AND PERSONALIZED NAPKIN RINGS

DESIGNER: **Kirsten Jones**

together is the best place to be

FALL CENTERPIECE AND PERSONALIZED NAPKIN RINGS

Look in your recycling bin for beautiful fall ideas for your table.

WHAT YOU'LL NEED MOD PODGE BASIC TOOL KIT (PAGE 18) ■ MOD PODGE SATIN ■ FOLKART ACRYLIC PAINTS: TERRA-COTTA, AZURE BLUE, TURNER'S YELLOW, AND SKY BLUE ■ FOLKART CHALKBOARD PAINT, BLACK ■ STICK OF WHITE CHALK ■ NO. 12 FLAT BRUSH ■ NO. 6 FLAT BRUSH ■ ASSORTED FALL-THEMED SCRAPBOOK PAPERS ■ 25 INCHES (63.5 CM) OF RED-AND-ORANGE TWINE (OR YOUR CHOICE OF COLORS) ■ MEDIUM COFFEE CAN ■ 4 TOILET PAPER TUBES (OR AS MANY AS YOU NEED FOR PLACE SETTINGS) ■ FOUR 3-INCH (7.6 CM) WOOD DISCS (OR AS MANY AS YOU NEED FOR PLACE SETTINGS) ■ SMALL WOOD BIRDHOUSE ■ WOOD CANDLESTICK ■ WOOD LEAF CUTOUT ■ SPANISH MOSS ■ HOT GLUE GUN AND GLUE STICKS

WHAT YOU'LL DO

BIRDHOUSE CENTERPIECE

1 Using FolkArt Acrylic Paints, first basecoat roof and sides of birdhouse Sky Blue. Then basecoat birdhouse base Terra-Cotta. Paint candlestick using assorted colors as shown in photo. Paint wood leaf Turner's Yellow. Allow all basecoated items to dry.

2 Cut out scrapbook papers to fit each section you will decoupage. Using the wood leaf as a pattern, cut out leaf in dotted yellow paper. A fall floral paper was used for the birdhouse body. We chose tan patterned paper to be used on the can.

3 Apply papers to each surface using Mod Podge Satin. Let dry completely.

4 Assemble the birdhouse centerpiece as shown in the photo on the previous page, using a hot glue gun to attach bottom of candlestick to bottom of coffee can and to attach top of candlestick to base of birdhouse. Hot-glue wood leaf to candlestick.

5 Complete with finishing touches. Tie twine to the can as an accent touch. Fill can with Spanish moss or dry floral grass.

NAPKIN RINGS

1 Cut four 1-inch (2.5 cm) strips from the variety of scrapbook papers. To plan the design, place the paper strip on the wood disc so that it is along one side (see photo). Then, turn upside down and, using the wood disc as a pattern, trace disc shape on paper. Trim the paper strip where it extends beyond the edges of the circle. Set aside for now.

2 Using the toilet paper tubes as patterns, cut out decorative papers to wrap around each roll.

3 Using Mod Podge Satin, apply the papers to each toilet paper tube and to the wood discs. Let dry completely.

4 Paint wood discs with two coats of FolkArt Chalkboard Paint in Black. Let dry between coats. Condition chalkboard painted areas by rubbing with white chalk before personalizing with a name.

5 Attach a wood disc to each toilet paper roll with hot glue.

6 Personalize each wood disc with white chalk.

MUMMY TREAT BOWL AND TREAT BAG

DESIGNER: **Sherrie Ragsdale**

MUMMY TREAT BOWL AND TREAT BAG

Spook all the guests at the party with this fun glow-in-the-dark mummy bowl with bonus treat bags.

WHAT YOU'LL NEED MOD PODGE BASIC TOOL KIT (PAGE 18) ◻ HALLOWEEN TEXT SCRAPBOOK PAPER ◻ MOD PODGE GLOW-IN-THE-DARK ◻ FOLKART ACRYLIC PAINT, LICORICE ◻ LARGE CLEAR PLASTIC BOWL ◻ CHEESECLOTH ◻ STYROFOAM EGGS ◻ SMALL WHITE CANVAS BAGS ◻ 1½-INCH (3.8 CM) STYROFOAM BALL ◻ HOT GLUE GUN AND GLUE STICKS

WHAT YOU'LL DO

MUMMY TREAT BOWL

1 Cut Halloween text scrapbook paper into squares. Set aside.

2 Apply four coats of Mod Podge Glow-in-the-Dark on the clear plastic bowl. Allow to dry between each coat. Mod Podge paper squares onto the outside of the clear bowl, using Mod Podge Glow-in-the-Dark, applying the paper squares so the text is facing toward the inside of the bowl. Cover the entire bowl with the text paper, and then add four coats of Mod Podge Glow-in-the-Dark over the paper, allowing layers to dry after each coat.

3 Cut the cheesecloth into strips. Using Mod Podge Glow-in-the-Dark, apply the cheesecloth strips to the outside of the bowl. Allow to dry.

4 Cut a Styrofoam egg in half and paint eyeballs in the center with FolkArt Acrylic Paint in Licorice. Glue foam eyeballs to the top of the bowl with hot glue. Cut more strips of cheesecloth and Mod Podge them across the eyes so that they are peeking out. Let dry.

TREAT BAGS

1 Cut bags to remove the handles.

2 Cut additional cheesecloth strips and fold at the edge of the bag; brush Mod Podge Glow-in-the-Dark on bag (A). Place cheesecloth strip over wet Mod Podge. Brush on additional Mod Podge Glow-in-the-Dark coats (B). Continue adding cheesecloth strips (C).

3 Cut a 1½-inch (3.8 cm) Styrofoam ball in half, and paint an eyeball on each half using FolkArt Acrylic Paint in Licorice.

4 Hot-glue Styrofoam eyes to the bag.

5 Cut more strips of cheesecloth to place across the eyes, to make it appear that they are peeking through.

6 Apply several coats of Mod Podge Glow-in-the-Dark. The more you add, the brighter it will glow; however, be sure to charge your glow-in-the-dark projects ahead of time. To charge, place project under direct light or in the sunlight for a couple of hours.

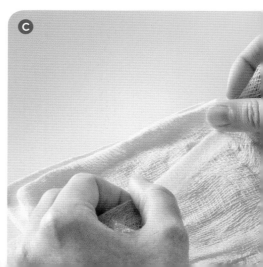

BURLAP- AND FABRIC-EMBELLISHED PUMPKINS

DESIGNERS: **Cathie Filian and Steve Piacenza**

BURLAP- AND FABRIC-EMBELLISHED PUMPKINS

Black, orange, and white fabrics are perfect for creating customized Halloween pumpkins with style. The fabrics can be cut into motifs or squares, or torn into strips. Add a little Glow-in-the-Dark Mod Podge for a spooky look at night.

WHAT YOU'LL NEED MOD PODGE BASIC TOOL KIT (PAGE 18) ☐ MOD PODGE FABRIC ☐ MOD PODGE GLOW-IN-THE-DARK ☐ MOD PODGE HARD COAT ☐ MOD PODGE MOD MELTER ☐ MOD PODGE MOD MELTS, SEA GLASS CLEAR ☐ MOD PODGE CRAFT MAT ☐ HALLOWEEN-COLORED FABRICS (IN MODELS: SOLID ORANGE, BLACK WITH WHITE DESIGN, WITH ORANGE MOTIF) ☐ FOAM PUMPKINS OR OTHER FAKE PUMPKINS (BLACK, WHITE, AND ORANGE) ☐ GLITTER ☐ DECORATIVE TRIM (OPTIONAL)

WHAT YOU'LL DO

MOTIF PUMPKIN (BLACK PUMPKIN IN MODEL)

1. Cut motifs from fabric.

2. Working on the craft mat, apply Mod Podge Fabric to the back of the cut fabric motif (A).

3. Position fabric motif on the pumpkin, and press with fingers to remove any air bubbles. Apply other motifs the same way (B). Allow to dry.

4. Topcoat with a layer of Mod Podge Hard Coat.

FABRIC STRIPS PUMPKIN (WHITE PUMPKIN IN MODEL)

1. Tear or cut fabric into strips.

2. Cut fabric strips into shorter strips that will fit the length of the pumpkin, from the neck of the stem to the bottom of the pumpkin.

3. Apply Mod Podge Fabric to the back of a strip and position the fabric strip on the pumpkin. Smooth with fingers to remove any air bubbles. Repeat around the pumpkin, spacing strips evenly (see photo). Allow to dry.

BURLAP PATCHWORK PUMPKIN (ORANGE PUMPKIN)

1. Cut the fabric into random-sized squares.

2. Working on a craft mat, apply Mod Podge Fabric to the wrong side of the burlap squares.

3. Position burlap squares on the pumpkin, overlapping slightly.

4. Continue adding burlap squares until the pumpkin is covered. Allow to dry.

5. Hot-glue decorative trim to outline features on jack-o'-lantern, if desired.

GLITTERING THE STEMS (FOR ALL)

1. Apply Mod Podge Hard Coat to the stem of the pumpkin. While wet, sprinkle glitter over the stem. Tap off the excess and allow to dry.

MAKE IT GLOW

1. Apply Mod Podge Glow-in-the-Dark over the entire pumpkin, or just over the fabric area to create a spooky glow-in-the-dark effect.

ADD TRIMS (ALL)

1. Hot-glue trim around the stems, if desired, and around features of jack-o'-lantern.

DECODEN HOLIDAY GIFT TIN

DESIGNERS: **Cathie Filian and Steve Piacenza**

DECODEN HOLIDAY GIFT TIN

Mod Podge Collage Clay is perfect for making faux snow on holiday projects. To add the extra sparkle, simply sprinkle ultra-fine white glitter over wet Mod Podge Collage Clay.

WHAT YOU'LL NEED MOD PODGE COLLAGE CLAY, VANILLA WHITE ☐ SQUARE COOKIE TIN ☐ ULTRA-FINE WHITE GLITTER ☐ MINI HOLIDAY HOUSE ☐ MINI TREES ☐ SMALL AND LARGE SNOWFLAKE EMBELLISHMENTS ☐ RHINESTONES ☐ FAUX PEARLS

WHAT YOU'LL DO

1 Using the star decorating tip on the Mod Podge Collage Clay Vanilla White bag, apply Mod Podge Vanilla White Collage Clay over the entire cookie tin lid, as if you were decorating a cake.

2 While Mod Podge Collage Clay Vanilla White is wet, sprinkle glitter over the entire lid.

3 Embed the holiday house and mini trees into the clay by pressing them in place while Mod Podge Collage Clay is still wet.

4 Embed the large snowflakes into the wet Mod Podge Collage Clay Vanilla White; then add the small snowflakes.

5 Continue adding accents by embedding pearls and rhinestones into the lid. Allow to dry overnight.

6 Apply Mod Podge Collage Clay Vanilla White to the side (or sides) of the box (A). Embed additional snowflakes, pearls, and rhinestone embellishments by pressing them into the clay (B). Allow to dry thoroughly before use. Dry time may take up to 7–10 days, depending on humidity and thickness of application.

"YOU WARM MY HEART" ORNAMENT

DESIGNER: **Debbie Saenz**

"YOU WARM MY HEART" ORNAMENT

I had so much fun creating a "snowstorm" with white paint and an old toothbrush as the base for this ornament, to showcase the warmth of love in the middle of a cold winter.

WHAT YOU'LL NEED MOD PODGE BASIC TOOL KIT (PAGE 18) ☐ MOD PODGE GLOSS ☐ FOLKART ACRYLIC PAINT, WICKER WHITE ☐ FOLKART EXTREME GLITTER, HOLOGRAM ☐ MOD PODGE WONDER GLUE ☐ DRILL AND DRILL BITS ☐ SCALLOPED WOOD PLAQUE ☐ BLUE-AND-WHITE SNOWFLAKE PAPER LARGE ENOUGH TO COVER FRONT OF PLAQUE ☐ PAINTER'S TAPE ☐ OLD TOOTHBRUSH ☐ DISTRESSING INK ☐ BLACK-AND-WHITE PHOTO ☐ 2-INCH (5.1 CM) WOOD SNOWFLAKE ☐ IRIDESCENT GLITTER ☐ RHINESTONES ☐ SNOWFLAKE-SHAPED RHINESTONES ☐ METAL TAG ☐ METAL STAMPING LETTERS AND HEART SYMBOL ☐ BLACK PERMANENT MARKER ☐ STEEL WOOL ☐ SANDPAPER ☐ 2 WHITE EYELETS (GROMMETS) ☐ SILVER CHAIN TO HANG PLAQUE ☐ 2 CLEAR GLASS BEADS ON SNOWFLAKE ORNAMENT AS EMBELLISHMENT ☐ 2 EYE PINS ☐ 2 LARGE JUMP RINGS

WHAT YOU'LL DO

1 Apply FolkArt Acrylic Paint in Wicker White to edges and back of wood plaque and snowflake.

2 Trace wood plaque shape onto back of snowflake paper. Cut out and adhere paper to front (unpainted side) of plaque with Mod Podge Gloss. Distress edges of photo with distressing ink and adhere photo at an angle on right side of ornament. Using sandpaper, remove any paper that extends beyond the edges of plaque when dry. Distress the edges with distressing ink. Apply a topcoat of Mod Podge Gloss over ornament. Allow to dry.

3 Apply a generous amount of Mod Podge Gloss to snowflake; while wet, pour glitter over snowflake, shake off. Repeat if necessary. Set aside to dry.

4 Cover faces on photo with painter's tape to protect it. Use an old paintbrush dipped in paint and flick FolkArt Acrylic Paint in Wicker White over the front of the plaque to create a snowy effect. Remove tape.

5 Paint plaque, up to the edges of the photo, with FolkArt Extreme Glitter Hologram. Allow to dry. Seal with a coat of Mod Podge Gloss.

6 With drill, make holes in upper corners of the plaque for hanging. Add eyelets.

7 Stamp metal tag with YOU WARM MY HEART, or use heart symbol stamp instead of word HEART, if desired. Fill letter crevices by tracing them with a black permanent marker. Polish off excess marker with steel wool.

8 Use Mod Podge Wonder Glue to attach metal tag, snowflake, and rhinestones to plaque.

9 Use eye pins for clear glass beads and attach to chain. Attach chain to ornament with jump rings.

BONUS PROJECT

FESTIVE HOT-AIR BALLOON ORNAMENT

I just knew there were more uses for papier-mâché Easter eggs! With a little modification, a colorful paper napkin, and Mod Podge, of course, an egg works perfectly as an adorable hot-air balloon ornament.

WHAT YOU'LL NEED MOD PODGE GLOSS ▫ FOLKART ACRYLIC PAINTS: WICKER WHITE AND DAFFODIL YELLOW ▫ PAPIER-MÂCHÉ EASTER EGG ▫ SMALL WOOD FLOWERPOT (FOR BASKET OF BALLOON) ▫ COLORFUL NAPKIN OR TISSUE PAPER ▫ COLORFUL RICKRACK AND TRIM ▫ EYE PIN (OPTIONAL) ▫ COLORFUL STRING ▫ HOT GLUE GUN AND GLUE STICKS ▫ CRAFT TAPE ▫ SCISSORS

WHAT YOU'LL DO

1 Cut off one end of Easter egg to create hot air balloon shape. Paint egg with FolkArt Acrylic Paint in Wicker White. Paint entire flowerpot using FolkArt Acrylic Paint in Daffodil Yellow.

2 Cut a circle from napkin or tissue paper that is big enough to overlap the balloon shape with some extra at the bottom. Separate and use only the top (decorative) ply of napkin. Make five or six wedge cuts into the paper circle, spaced around the circle, from the outside to the center, keeping a half-inch (1.3 cm) circle in the center uncut. Apply Mod Podge Gloss to the egg and place center of paper circle on what will be the top of balloon; smooth down each wedge with fingers, being careful not to rip the paper. Fold excess paper around bottom edges of egg shape, tucking inside, and securing with Mod Podge Gloss. Allow to dry. Seal with a coat of Mod Podge Gloss.

3 Make a hole in top center of balloon. Insert eye pin and feed string through eye pin; create a loop and knot for hanging.

4 For the ropes of the balloon, use hot glue to attach six short strings, spaced around circle, inside opening of hot-air balloon; and also attach them to outside of flowerpot "basket."

5 Adhere trim around flowerpot basket with hot glue. Adhere rickrack trims around bottom of balloon and bottom of basket with Mod Podge Gloss. Let dry before using.

BONUS PROJECT

WINDOW OF LOVE ORNAMENT

This adorable little window is picture perfect, showcasing lots of love. And of course, it can be personalized by adding the year or a family name to the heart.

WHAT YOU'LL NEED MOD PODGE BASIC TOOL KIT (PAGE 18) ☐ MOD PODGE GLOSS ☐ MOD PODGE DIMENSIONAL MAGIC, CLEAR ☐ FOLKART ACRYLIC PAINTS: METALLIC AQUAMARINE AND VINTAGE WHITE ☐ DOLLHOUSE WINDOW ☐ BLACK AND WHITE PHOTOCOPIES OF FAMILY MEMBERS SIZED TO FIT THE WINDOW OPENINGS ☐ 1 SHEET OF DECORATIVE PATTERNED PAPER ☐ 1 SHEET OF MUSIC PAPER (FOR HEART) ☐ DISTRESSING INK ☐ CHIPBOARD (OR BACK OF CEREAL BOX) ☐ 1½-INCH (3.8 CM) WOOD HEART ☐ 1-INCH (2.5 CM) WOOD HEART ☐ GLITTERED RHINESTONE HEART, SMALLER THAN 1-INCH (2.5 CM) WOOD HEART ☐ RED RIBBON ☐ 6 PEARL RHINESTONES ☐ RED-AND-WHITE LACE TRIM ☐ SMALL **L O V E** RED-GLITTERED LETTERS OR SUBSTITUTE PLAIN LETTERS AND GLITTER USING MOD PODGE GLOSS ☐ 17 RED RHINESTONES ☐ 2 JUMP RINGS ☐ 2 SCREW EYES (TO HANG HEART FROM WINDOW) ☐ SILVER CHAIN (3 TO 4 LINKS) ☐ DECORATIVE CORD FOR HANGING WINDOW ☐ DRILL AND DRILL BIT TO MAKE HOLES FOR SCREW EYES ☐ JEWELRY PLIERS TO OPEN JUMP RINGS ☐ MOD PODGE WONDER GLUE ☐ HOT GLUE GUN AND GLUE STICKS ☐ SANDPAPER

WHAT YOU'LL DO

1 Paint edges and front of window and largest heart with FolkArt Acrylic Paint in Metallic Aquamarine. Paint 1-inch (2.5 cm) heart using FolkArt Acrylic Paint in Vintage White.

2 Adhere decorative papers to window and hearts (see photo for reference). The large heart takes decorative patterned paper, and the smaller heart takes music-patterned paper. Sand off all extra paper that extends beyond the edges with sandpaper. Distress the edges of windows with distressing ink, and seal with a coat of Mod Podge Gloss. Allow to dry.

3 Measure and cut chipboard to cover back of window frame where photos will be. Trace window openings onto chipboard, and use Mod Podge Gloss to adhere photocopies on chipboard in the window opening areas. Adhere chipboard to back of window with Mod Podge Gloss. Paint back of chipboard using FolkArt Acrylic Paint in Metallic Aquamarine.

4 Drill a hole in center bottom of window, and twist in screw eye to hang heart.

5 Glue 1-inch (2.5 cm) heart over the largest heart using Mod Podge Wonder Glue. Create a hole in top center of the largest heart for screw eye to hang hearts. Attach red rhinestones around largest heart, and glue rhinestone heart in center of 1-inch (2.5 cm) heart. Hang hearts with chain and jump rings from bottom of window. (Open jump rings to thread them through screw eyes, and then close them.)

6 Using Mod Podge Wonder Glue, arrange and glue down LOVE letters, lace, red bow, and pearls on window. (See photo for guidance.) Let dry.

7 Fill window openings over photos with Mod Podge Dimensional Magic Clear, and set aside to dry.

8 With hot glue, adhere cord on back of window for hanging.

HOLIDAY GIFT TAGS

DESIGNER: **Julieta Martinez**

HOLIDAY GIFT TAGS

Recycle your cereal boxes to make your own gift tags.

WHAT YOU'LL NEED MOD PODGE BASIC TOOL KIT (PAGE 18) ■ MOD PODGE PAPER ■ CEREAL BOX ■ TAG-SHAPED PUNCH [A 3-INCH (7.6 CM) SCALLOPED PUNCH IS USED IN THE MODEL] ■ SMALLER PUNCH (FOR "TO" AND "FROM" TAGS) (OPTIONAL) ■ ASSORTED HOLIDAY SCRAPBOOK PAPER OR GIFT WRAP ■ CARDBOARD OR HEAVY SCRAPBOOK PAPER ■ SMALL HOLE PUNCH ■ CORD (COTTON, HEMP, KNITTING YARN, OR CORD OF PREFERENCE) ■ TEMPLATE (PAGE 231)

WHAT YOU'LL DO

1 Cut the cereal box open along the sides, forming one flat sheet.

2 Cut tags by punching through cereal box with scalloped circle punch (A), or use a scissors and pattern provided in the Template section of book.

3 Use the same punch to create additional template shapes from scrapbook paper or giftwrap.

4 Brush Mod Podge Paper onto the cardboard tag (B).

5 Mod Podge the paper tag to the cardboard tag. Repeat for back side of tag.

6 Cut a piece of cardboard in any shape you prefer, using a small punch or scissors, and glue it over the paper on the tag front, for a place to write the "to" and "from" messages on the tag.

7 Make a hole on the top of the large tag, using the single-hole punch.

8 Cut a piece of cord approximately 5 inches (12.7 cm) long, fold it double, and insert it through the hole of the tag; make a knot to secure.

CD WREATH

DESIGNER: ***Vivienne Wagner***

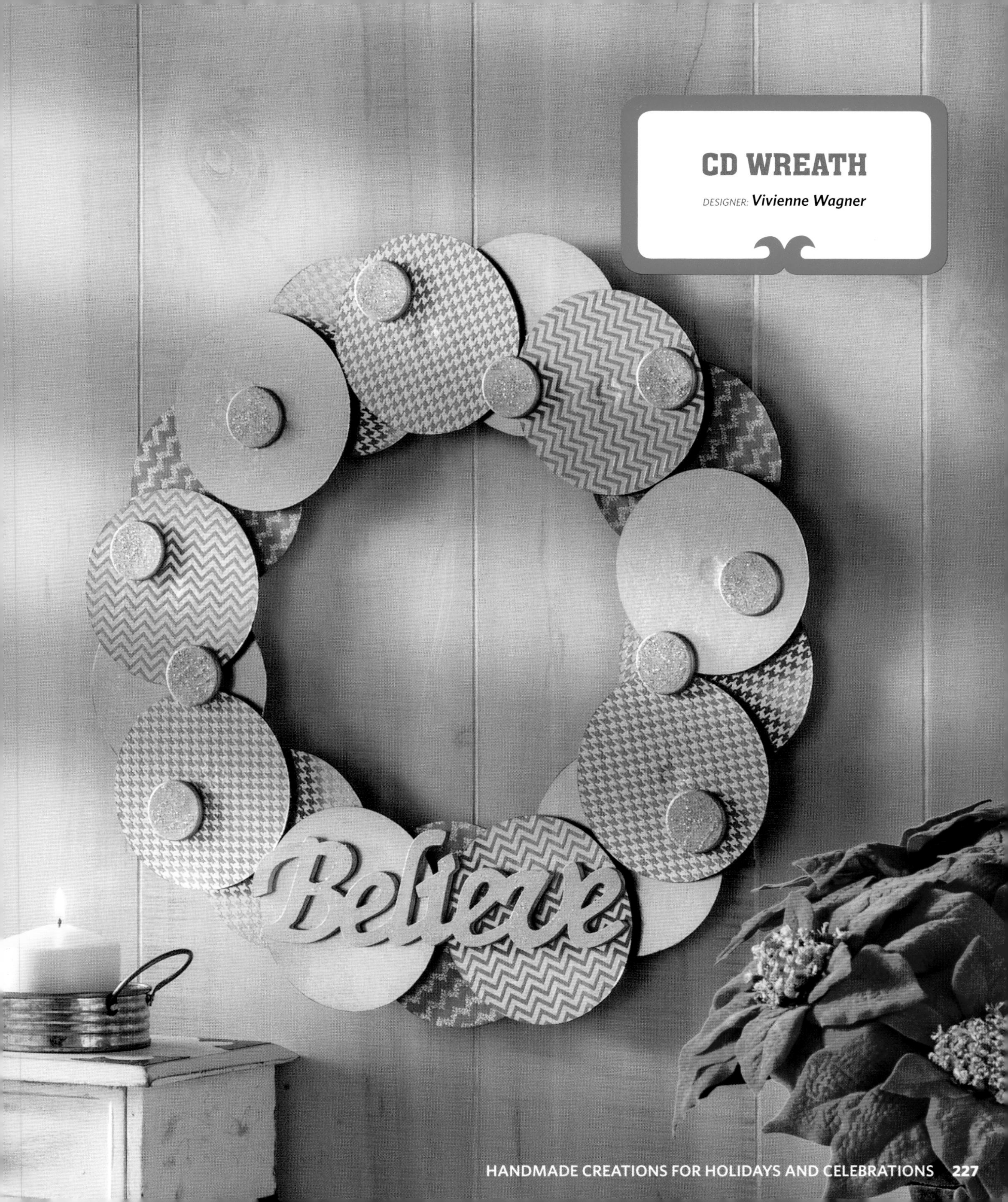

CD WREATH

CDs are giving way to digital downloads, but there is still lots of life left in them.

WHAT YOU'LL NEED MOD PODGE BASIC TOOL KIT (PAGE 18) ☐ MOD PODGE GLOSS ☐ MOD PODGE EXTREME GLITTER ☐ 18 COMPACT DISCS (CDS) ☐ 18-INCH (45.7 CM) DIAMETER FLORAL OR CRAFT RING ☐ 18-INCH (45.7 CM) LENGTH OF RIBBON ☐ TEN 1½-INCH (3.8 CM) WOODEN DISCS ☐ 5 SHEETS OF DECORATIVE PAPER, COORDINATING COLORS AND PATTERNS, EACH 12 x 12 INCHES (30.5 x 30.5 CM) ☐ ACRYLIC PAINT IN A COORDINATING COLORTO PAPERS ☐ MOD PODGE WONDER GLUE ☐ CUTOUT WOOD TEXT (WELCOME, HAPPY HOLIDAYS ... PHRASE OF YOUR CHOICE)

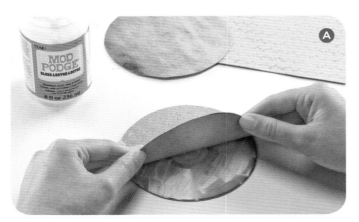

WHAT YOU'LL DO

1 Using a pencil, trace the CDs on the back of the decorative papers and cut out 19 paper circles.

2 Apply a coat of Mod Podge Gloss to each CD and carefully adhere the paper circle over it, taking care to smooth out any air bubbles (A). Repeat for all 17 remaining CDs.

3 Let dry, then trim any excess paper with craft knife. Apply a topcoat of either Mod Podge Gloss or Mod Podge Extreme Glitter, depending upon the desired look, and let dry.

4 Tie the length of ribbon around the floral ring to create a loop, and arrange 9 of the Mod Podged CDs in a circle on top of the ring. Once placement has been decided, apply Mod Podge Wonder Glue to the back of each CD, one at a time, and adhere to the ring (B).

5 Paint the wooden discs and wood text cutouts with the acrylic paint and let dry.

6 Apply adhesive to the backs of 9 of the painted discs and place them on top of the bottom layer of CDs, right where the curve of each circle touches the one next to it.

7 Add a small amount of Mod Podge Wonder Glue to the top of each disc and gently press a CD on top of it, creating a second, offset layer of CDs.

8 Paint wooden text cut out and let dry.

9 Apply Mod Podge Extreme Glitter over the tops of the remaining discs (C) and over the text cutout.

10 Apply adhesive to the back of the remaining disks and the text cutout, and place on the wreath, pressing firmly but gently to adhere. Let dry before hanging.

ARTFUL TREE CANVAS

DECORATOR PATTERNED PAPER BOX SET

PAGE 117 – Enlarge by 225%

PAGE 191 – Enlarge by 225%

FAUX CORK INLAY TABLE

FABRIC DECOUPAGED TERRA-COTTA FLOWERPOTS

PAGE 41 – Enlarge by 225%

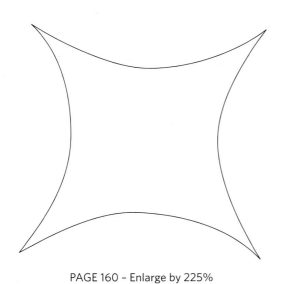

PAGE 160 – Enlarge by 225%

TEMPLATES

GARDENING DOLL ALTERED BIRDHOUSE

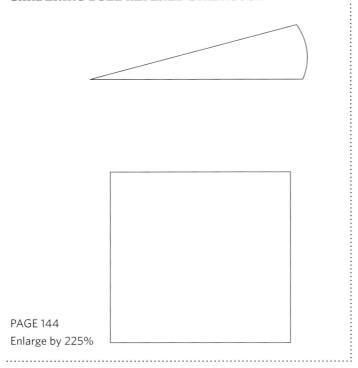

PAGE 144
Enlarge by 225%

HOME IS WHERE THE HEART IS

PAGE 110 – Enlarge by 225%

SAFARI ANIMAL BIRTHDAY PARTY

PAGE 68
Enlarge by 225%

HOLIDAY GIFT TAGS

PAGE 225 – Enlarge by 225%

ARTFUL GLAM JEWELRY

PAGE 133 – Enlarge by 225%

FAUX OILCLOTH FLOWER BROOCH

PAGE 125
Enlarge by 225%

NO-SEW DECORATIVE PILLOWS

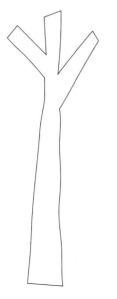

PAGE 49 – Enlarge by 225%

VALENTINE DAY BOX

Be Mine

PAGE 202 – Enlarge by 225%

NO-SEW DECORATIVE PILLOWS

WHIMSICAL BIRD MOBILE

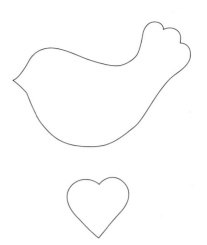

PAGE 104 – Enlarge by 225%

PAINT-CHIP WALL ART

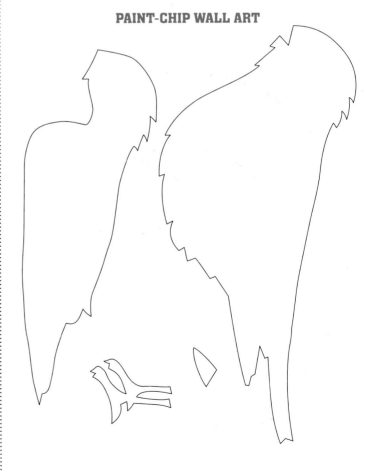

PAGE 49 – Enlarge by 225%

PAGE 114 – Enlarge by 225%

PAGE 114 – Enlarge by 225%

CONTRIBUTING DESIGNERS

Amy Anderson is the author of *Mod Podge Rocks!* She currently runs three successful craft blogs with a combined one million+ page views per month. She also designs creative projects for large brands and writes craft books. Find out more about Amy by visiting http://www.modpodgerocksblog.com.

Paul Bowman founded Design Samaritan to help others and save valuable resources from the landfill. This social enterprise gives new life to old furniture through design. Sales enable donations of furniture to families transitioning from homelessness. His work is featured at http://www.designsamaritan.com.

Maggie Brereton created the inspiring website *Smashed Peas and Carrots*, where she shares her love for all things DIY, including sewing, craft tutorials, recipes, and projects for children. Find out more about Maggie by visiting www.smashedpeasandcarrots.com.

David Cheaney is a Los Angeles, California-based crafter who owes his entire empire to Mod Podge. You can follow his adventures at http://www.cheltenhamroad.wordpress.com or drop by his Etsy store: http://www.cheltenhamroad.etsy.com.

Carol Cook is a self-taught paper and mixed media artist. She loves all things Mod Podge and chocolate. Carol creates items for her home, friends, and family.

Candie Cooper is a jewelry designer with a passion for bold colors who loves twisting materials until they sing! She has authored four jewelry how-to publications with Lark Crafts: *Earringology*, *Necklacecology*, *Metalworking 101 for Beaders*, and *Felted Jewelry*. She has appeared on Jewelry Television's *Jewel School* and the PBS series *Beads Baubles and Jewels*. See her work at http://www.candiecooper.com.

Andrea Currie is a creative industry professional, author, and lover of all things sparkly. She and her husband, Cliff, share a popular blog about their adventures in crafting, DIY, and home improvement, *Hand Make My Day*: http://handmakemyday.com/.

Rachel Faucett is the mother of five ridiculously cute children and has enough creative energy to run circles around them. When she's not bringing her dreams to life with giant frog costumes, neon glow stick signs, and soft-enough-to-snuggle yarn mosaics, you can find Rachel traveling the world for inspiration or throwing awesome DIY parties at her farm just outside Atlanta, Georgia. Named one of the top 20 most influential Pinterest users by *Business Insider*, the author/designer also keeps herself busy designing for brands such as Anthropologie and Pottery Barn Kids.

Cathie Filian and Steve Piacenza are designers, Emmy-nominated lifestyle hosts, and bestselling book authors. They have been featured on HGTV, DIY, Food Network, Rachael Ray, and in *Real Simple*, *Better Homes and Gardens*, and *HGTV Magazine*. Their products are available nationwide at top craft retailers. Learn more about this crafty duo at http://www.cathieandsteve.com.

Stacie Grissom is a craft-loving Indiana girl living in New York City! When she's not toting around a loaded Nikon or working on her blog, *Stars for Streetlights*, she is making a large mess in her living room. For more on her and her work, see http://www.starsforstreetlights.com.

Kirsten Jones has been crafting for the past 25 ears. She specializes in whimsical and folksy paintings. For inspiration, she attends and exhibits at art shows across the country. She's had her work published in numerous craft books and has appeared on multiple DIY and home shopping shows, including QVC

Julie Lewis has been a designer and crafter for over 25 years with a BFA in graphic design. She never seems to run out of creative inspiration when surrounded daily by amazing people. Her experience working within an eclectic list of industries has helped to hone her creative approach to work and life. Greeting cards, industrial advertising, toys, graphic design, and the craft industry, to name a few, have afforded Julie the opportunity to bring unique talents to her satisfying job as designer and design manager at PLAID Enterprises, Inc. See her work at http://www.stellalola.etsy.com.

Julieta Martinez is a fashion, lifestyle, and DIY blogger. She is a mother to two boys who occasionally help with her projects. You can always find Julieta on her blog at http://www.vjuliet.com.

Mark Montano is a hardcore DIYer and TV host who has published 11 craft books and starred in five home décor series. Currently Mark can be seen hosting *Make Your Mark* for public television. Find out more about Mark and his work at his website: http://www.MarkMontano.com.

Holli Nutter is a third-generation crafter who has worked for PLAID Enterprises, Inc., as designer, both freelance and in-house, for approximately 20 years. She has crafted thousands of finished samples for everything from packaging to trade show props. Her favorite mediums are FolkArt Acrylics and Mod Podge. Holli is also a Level 2 One Stroke Certified Instructor!

Sherrie Ragsdale is a creative person whose life experiences help her grow and continually add unique skills to her rewarding job as designer at PLAID Enterprises, Inc. Sherrie's amazing two boys inspire and challenge her on a daily basis to approach life with a renewed creative spirit. The combination of Sherrie's passions, thrifting, and building results in a special ability to combine everyday objects into objects of art.

Debbie Saenz lives in Atlanta, Georgia, with her family. She has designed hundreds of projects as a freelance designer for PLAID Enterprises, Inc., using Mod Podge, but she also enjoys many other art forms. Visit her Etsy shop at http://www.debbiesaenz.etsy.com, her Facebook page at http://www.facebook.com/A Creative Life, or her blog at http://www.debbiesaenz.typepad.com, where she shares *A Creative Life*.

Walter Silva is a Mod Podge guru and DIY guy living in Providence, Rhode Island. He loves making things with new and repurposed items. Join him on his adventures via his blog: http://waltersilvaart.blogspot.com.

Kristen Turner is the creator of the fashion and lifestyle how-to blog *Miss Kris*. It's the modern-day girl's guide to surviving life fabulously on a budget. It's affordable luxury at its best: http://www.MissKrisTurner.com.

Vivienne Wagner writes the popular blog *The V Spot*, where she shares crafts, DIY projects, recipes, and funny stories. Her projects have been featured on sites such as *Apartment Therapy*, *Lifehacker*, and *Fox News Magazine* as well as some of the most popular craft and lifestyle blogs around. If Erma Bombeck and MacGyver had a love child, that child might have been a little bit like her! Check out her work at http://www.thevspotblog.com/.

Laura Whitlow has a vision for seeing beauty in discarded items (can we say trash?) and created Rethunk Junk by Laura, a company that repurposes furniture and accessories and has developed a successful furniture paint line. When without a paintbrush in her hand, Laura is spending time with family (five kids and a very supportive spouse), playing piano, or reading. Her work is featured on the website http://www.rethunkjunkbylaura.com.

Chris Williams is happiest when she is designing and creating. While decorative painting is her first love, a close second is decoupaging using Mod Podge. Chris has authored many how-to craft books while working in the craft industry for years traveling, teaching, and sharing basic crafting how-tos. In her position at PLAID Enterprises, Inc., she is responsible for all educational content. Follow Chris's crafting how-to blog posts at *PLAID Online*, http://www.plaidonline.com/blog/, or on Pinterest at http://www.pinterest.com/cwilliams1023/.

ABOUT PLAID®

In 1976, PLAID® founder, David Cunningham set out to create "a diversified, yet synergistic company that would provide the most complete, comprehensive programs available to market and sell craft products."

His dream has become a reality! Today, PLAID® Enterprises, Inc., has grown to become one of the world's largest, most diverse manufacturers of creative do-it-yourself products, and the PLAID® family of brands are among the most recognized and desired craft products in the world. PLAID®'s portfolio includes FolkArt®, Apple Barrel®, Delta®, Martha Stewart Crafts®, Bucilla®, and Mod Podge®, a favorite since 1967.

This industry has a very bright future, as the Makers Movement and DIY culture continue to gain momentum worldwide and PLAID® continues to be at the forefront of crafting and enriching people's lives.

ACKNOWLEDGMENTS

Thank you to our contributing designers; to Steve Carrell, photographer; and to the PLAID® Production Team: Anna Teal, hand model; Chris Myer Williams, content curator; Rena Williams, project manager; Connie Lanham, brand manager; Andrea Henfield, category director.

INDEX

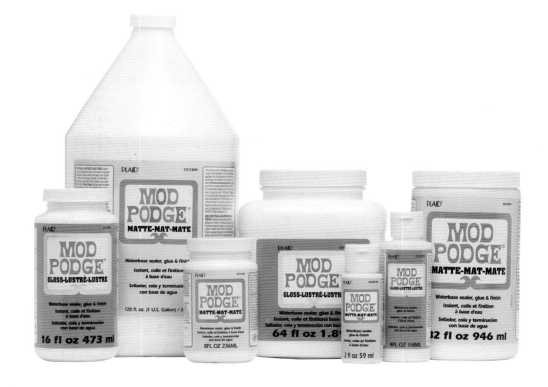